LISTENING BETWEEN THE LINES:

THINKING MISSIOLOGICALLY ABOUT ROMANIAN CULTURE

Cameron D. Armstrong

LISTENING BETWEEN THE LINES:

THINKING MISSIOLOGICALLY ABOUT ROMANIAN CULTURE

Cameron D. Armstrong

FaithVenture Media

Listening Between the Lines: Thinking Missiologically About Romanian Culture
Written by Cameron D. Armstrong
Copyright © 2018 by Cameron D. Armstrong

ISBN 978-606-94447-8-8

FaithVenture Media - *www.faithventuremedia.com*
Târgu Mureş, România

"And without faith it is impossible to please him, for whoever would draw near to God must believe that he exists and that he rewards those who seek him." Hebrews 11:6

Descrierea CIP a Bibliotecii Naţionale a României
ARMSTRONG, CAMERON D.
   Listening between the lines : thinking missiologically about
Romanian culture / Cameron D. Armstrong. - Târgu Mureş :
FaithVenture Media, 2018
   Conţine bibliografie
   ISBN 978-606-94447-8-8

2

Response to *Listening Between the Lines*

The moment Cameron Armstrong arrived in Bucharest, Romania, I was impressed with his eagerness to immerse himself in language and cultural acquisition, as well as his passionate zeal for sharing the gospel. His field experience and diligent research will be a valuable resource to any long-term or short-term missionary. Cameron has done the missiological world a great favor by sharing his keen insight for developing deep and meaningful cross-cultural relationships.

Dr. Richard C. Clark
Senior Pastor, Indian Springs Baptist Church
Laurel, Mississippi
Former IMB Missionary to Romania

For nearly three decades a freed and democratic Romania has been the locus of a flurry of missions activity, some more helpful than others. In this volume, Cameron Armstrong provides an astute missiological framework for greater impact through genuine culturally informed relationships. If you've ever worked in Eastern Europe, you'd do well to read, learn and apply the principles herein.

Dr. George G. Robinson
Associate Professor of Missions & Evangelism
Headrick Chair of World Missions
Southeastern Baptist Theological Seminary

Cameron Armstrong recognizes what few long and short-term cross-cultural Christian workers do – relationships really matter in ministry. While cast in the Romanian context, insights and implications go far beyond its borders. Timely and timeless.

Tom Steffen, D.Miss.
Professor of Intercultural Studies
Cook School of Intercultural Studies
Biola University

Cameron's writing is informed by a unique combination of vast academic knowledge achieved in the USA and over six years of experience on the field in Romania. It has been a great blessing to have the Armstrongs among us; not only as American missionaries, but also as dear members of our Romanian church family in Bucharest.

Ben Mogoş, Th.M.
Founding Pastor
Agapia Baptist Church
Bucharest, Romania

Cameron Armstrong examines and wrestles, through a missiological lens, how the gospel ministers to the Romanian people at a personal, emotional, and societal level. By looking at these multiple aspects and spheres of Romanian culture, he engages and challenges the Romanian and non-Romanian reader to think missiologically about how to minister more holistically, no matter which country or culture they are in.

Jeff Cardell
Long-Term Missionary
Adventures in Missions
Timişoara, Romania

*In **Listening Between the Lines**, Cameron Armstrong makes a valuable contribution to effective, contextualized ministry. His passion for the gospel, highly relational research, humble and gracious spirit, and experience in Romania all are connected to provide a practical and insightful resource that will be helpful to those who send, go, and receive cross-cultural workers among Romanian people and others.*

Preston Pearce, Ph.D.
Theological Education Strategist for Eurasia
International Mission Board, SBC
Prague, Czech Republic

Cameron writes from personal experience and daily interaction with these cultural realities. This work is applicable and accessible to both the anthropologist and layman alike.

Dwight Poggemiller
Leader for Training and Development
Greater Europe Mission
Timișoara, Romania

This is the book to read before doing a short or long-term mission to Romania. Important insights on the Romanian culture and how to apply the gospel to this particular context. I would also recommend this book to Romanian evangelicals in order for them to be effective in sharing the gospel with their friends, family, and colleagues.

Ionut Popescu
Team Leader
CRU
Bucharest, Romania

Having ministered in Romania over more than two decades, I've experienced a full range of cultural experiences. Cameron Armstrong's insightful work on aspects of the church and culture in this country is well-grounded and generous. He's helped me to fall in love once again with the richness of our Romanian cultural context!

Dave Cox
City Team Leader
EFCA ReachGlobal
Bucharest, Romania

To Jessica, beloved bride, loving mother, steady helpmate, dearest friend

Books Published by FaithVenture Media

Using Technology for Your Church (2017)

Providence: God's Care for the Lost Sheep (2017)

Patience Before Marriage (2017)

Thirty Days of Thanksgiving (2017)

Listening Between the Lines (2018)

To find out more about FaithVenture Media's books, visit www.faithventuremedia.com/list-of-books

TABLE OF CONTENTS

INTRODUCTION: MY JOURNEY i

CHAPTER ONE: SOCIAL ANTHROPOLOGY AND MISSIOLOGY IN CONVERSATION: A CASE STUDY FROM ROMANIA 1

CHAPTER TWO: LEADERSHIP PATTERNS IN ROMANIA AND FUTURE MISSIOLOGICAL IMPLICATIONS 27

CHAPTER THREE: ROMANIAN-AMERICAN IDENTITY NEGOTIATION: A CASE STUDY IN INTERCULTURAL COMMUNICATION 53

CHAPTER FOUR: EDUCATION IN EASTERN ORTHODOXY 85

CHAPTER FIVE: ORTHODOX BACKGROUND BELIEVERS: LISTENING AND LEARNING 97

CHAPTER SIX: HONOR AND SHAME: CROSS-CURRENTS IN ROMANIAN CULTURE 117

CHAPTER SEVEN: TOWARDS A SUSTAINABLE MENTORING MODEL IN THE ROMANIAN BIBLE COLLEGE 145

INTRODUCTION:
MY JOURNEY

"Play soccer and share the gospel." That phrase is really all I remember from the booklet I'd received from my college's missions fair concerning the upcoming spring mission trip to Romania. The phrase caught my eye and I thought, "Well, I'm not really sure where Romania is, but I can do that!" And so it was that six months later I discovered my love for sharing Christ with Romanians.

I was born into a solidly Christian home where my mom and dad shared the gospel with me from my earliest days. At the age of four, however, death became real to me when I suffered a massive head injury due to a car accident. During my month or so of hospitalization, the doctors were convinced I would never walk or talk again. But God had different plans for me. After several weeks in a coma, God restored my ability to walk and talk.

More than that, my dad showed me that God had given me a taste of my mortality. One day, my dad said, I too will stand before God's throne and answer for the faith (or lack thereof) in my own heart. On that day, he explained, I cannot point to my father or mother's faith or the number of times I went to church. At the tender age of five, then, I clearly understood my sin before God, my inability to save myself, and my need for Christ's saving grace. I have not looked back since.

I suppose my first true overseas experience was living in Japan. My dad worked for Nissan for most of his career, and because of that we spent eighteen months in Yokohama when I was in third and fourth grades. I attended an international school and would often dream of the diverse homelands of my classmates. We also vacationed in Singapore, Malaysia, and the island of Saipan.

I chose to attend a Christian college in Tennessee called Union University, affiliated with the Southern Baptist Convention. Growing up, our family had attended a Southern Baptist church, but that didn't mean much to me at the time. So when the opportunity came to go to Romania, I didn't realize that the International Mission Board missionaries we worked with would one day become my colleagues. But now I'm getting ahead of myself.

That week in early April 2005 in Eastern Romania changed my life. Even though I'd always been rather quiet and shy, I volunteered to stand up in front of churches and share my testimony or devotion. I took the lead in sharing the gospel inside people's homes. I learned some Romanian words. It was fun and made me feel alive.

What I loved the most about that first trip, though, was worshipping with Romanian (and Roma or "gypsy") Christians. I remember clearly standing in one Roma church near the town of Braila, sweating because the pastor had stuck me next to the wooden stove that served as a heater. The worship song was vibrant and every hand in the room was raised. I thought, "I don't know if I can do anything for these people, but I just want to be around them."

So when the opportunity came for me to return the next year for the whole summer, I took it. And again I loved every minute of it. Preaching, teaching, and sharing the gospel daily *did not feel like work to me.* I returned after that summer aflame for missions, telling everyone who asked how God used me in Romania. I would eventually serve three summers in Romania (Cluj, Bucharest, and Timişoara).

A year after graduating from college, I realized the time was right to enter seminary full time and pursue mission work. I attended what I believe is one of the most missions-minded seminaries of our day, Southeastern Baptist Theological Seminary in Wake Forest, NC. The seminary has a close relationship with the International Mission Board (IMB) and regularly hosts weekends where interested seminarians can delve deeper into potentially serving with IMB. In 2010, I was disappointed that there were no IMB jobs listed for Romania, but I thought, "Hey, there are all these other church planting needs in India and South Asia. I'm single and have nothing to lose, so why not." Retrospectively speaking, that was not a wise nor prayerful decision, and I have to thank professors like George Robinson for helping me see that. Besides, there were other factors on the horizon.

I met my wife in 2009, but it was not until I'd started the process for serving in India that the Lord opened my eyes to Jessica as a possible mate. We got along swimmingly, as they say, and about a month after we started dating I knew I wanted to marry her (I waited a few more months to ask her, though). I stopped the process for India, and one might say I began the process for Jessica. We married in July 2011 and that fall began the process of applying with IMB.

It is truly amazing how the Lord works. Jessica had not considered missions until dating me, so it was all quite new for her. So we decided to pursue a two-year program with IMB called Journeyman. At the Journeyman conference, I was absolutely shocked to see a job on the books for church planting work in Bucharest, Romania. Naturally we felt the most comfortable about this job, and after skyping with our potential supervisors, Richard and Wanda Clark, IMB approved us to take the position. To recap, then, the way to Romania was shut for me as a bachelor, but wide open for me as a married man. After our two-year Journeyman term, we felt God calling us to stay in Bucharest as long-term missionaries. I cannot thank God enough for providing me a helpmate for this missionary life.

To date, we have served two terms in Bucharest. This places us squarely at six years with IMB in Romania. Although our roles, life situation, and team dynamics have changed, God has shown himself steadfast and faithful. We have made dear friends with the Romanian people and count it an honor to learn from them.

In 2014, my IMB supervisors graciously approved me to apply to the PhD Intercultural Education program at Biola University, the Cook School of Intercultural Studies. Impressed by several factors such as the faculty's careers as missionary scholars, the modular format for classes, the ethnic diversity among both students and faculty, and the unwavering commitment to biblical inerrancy, Biola seemed a perfect fit. Now, in 2018, I have completed my coursework and am entering the dissertation phase.

What follows is a compilation of several class papers I wrote during my time at Biola. Every professor wisely advised us to apply our learning to our ministry context. Another wonderful gift from God in these assignments is the push to qualitative research, which uses verbal data gleaned from personal, face-to-face interviews. The following seven essays take this qualitative approach. Although the essays were written at different points over the last several years and can largely standalone, the desire for contextualization brings cohesion. My overall hope is to give an "insider" view of Romanian culture so that Western missionaries like me will actually learn from the source: from Romanians themselves. The men and women whose stories are recorded in this book are all friends I have met over the years, although I have changed their names to protect anonymity.

In the thirteen years since I began serving in Romania, I have found that many churches from the

Global West, especially the United States, often send both short and long term teams to Romania. For example, a quick Google search of "short term mission trips to Romania" yields 515,000 results. While the Body of Christ should rejoice that not only so many Westerners have the opportunity to serve God in Romania but that so many Romanians might hear the saving message of the gospel, there is real danger in not understanding the culture into which a missionary (even a week-long missionary) is going. Missiologists call this delicate work of sharing the gospel in culturally-appropriate ways "contextualization." This book is one resource to guide conversations for ongoing contextualization beyond "What kind of food do they eat?" or "What kind of clothes do they wear?" Lord willing, Romanian and Western pastors and missionaries, both those sending and going, and even those receiving them, will benefit from such dialogue.

My purpose in these pages is not to give definitive answers to cultural questions or to claim that I have found "the best way forward" for ministry in Romania. Actually, I have many more questions than answers. Thankfully, though, this book is a testimony to the fact that all Christians, whether from Romania or elsewhere, are meant to wrestle with these questions together.

One final note is that, while Romania as a whole is under consideration, Bucharest and Baptists receive specific attention. I make no apology for that; I have researched and written about that which I know and love. I live in Bucharest, teach at the Baptist seminary, and work with Romanian Baptist churches to catalyze further church planting efforts. I do hope, though, that my analysis may assist other groups and regions as we take the gospel to all corners of the globe.

To delineate an exhaustive list of men and women worthy of thanks is virtually impossible. Thank you to all the Romanian men, women, and children who lovingly teach me about the Romanian culture. Thank you to all the pastors and professors, and missionaries who discipled me, believed in me, challenged me, and continue to encourage and push me. A special thanks goes to the ministry leaders who endorsed this book. Thank you to my parents who shared Christ with me, consistently model a godly marriage, and pray incessantly for my family. Thank you to Bill for the original idea to put this book together. Thanks to Mircea for brilliantly designing the cover of this (my first) book, and for Jeremy, Magda, and FaithVenture Media for taking a chance on me. Thanks to my sister, Kendall, for her amazing editing powers. And thank you, of course, to my beloved bride, Jessica, for putting up with all this writing and rewriting and talking about Romania. I dedicate this volume to you, my love.

Soli Deo gloria,
Cameron D. Armstrong
Bucharest, Romania

Cameron D. Armstrong

CHAPTER ONE:

SOCIAL ANTHROPOLOGY AND MISSIOLOGY IN CONVERSATION:

A CASE STUDY FROM ROMANIA

Understanding social organization is essential in constructing ministry strategy, yet even more so when working cross-culturally. Because ministry at its most basic level involves engaging and motivating people with the revealed truths of the Bible, greater knowledge of the life and nature of the people group one is seeking to engage can only assist in the formulation of ministry models. As an American missionary living and working in Bucharest, I am keenly aware that such knowledge of Romanian culture is best attained through in-depth interviews that depict, as much as possible, an insider (emic) perspective of Romanian social organization. For this reason, I greatly appreciated conducting six stimulating interviews with Samuel. Samuel has lived his entire life in the city of Bucharest, and his wife is currently the language teacher for my wife and me. While Samuel's views may not be indicative of the entire population of Romania, our time together yielded enough data to help identify trends and tendencies. All interviews were given entirely in the Romanian language, which allowed Samuel freedom to speak at his own leisure in his native tongue about social organization in Romania.[1]

This chapter will be divided into two broad sections: theoretical and practical. Utilizing both thoughts from Samuel and published anthropological concepts, I will first explain Romanian ideas concerning the following: how close relationships may be viewed as networks, common interests and ambitions, and analysis of Romanian social identity. In the latter half of the chapter, I will demonstrate how this data may be used in future ministry strategy, both for church planting purposes and further cultural research. Before delving into the social concepts, however, it is helpful to briefly understand some basic preliminary information about the historical context in which our cultural informant lives.

The Cultural Informant and His World

As mentioned above, Samuel has lived his entire life in Bucharest, the capital city of Romania. With a metropolitan population of roughly 2 million, Bucharest is by far the nation's largest city. Bucharest is a quite modern city, with a fully operational public transit system and developing business sector, making it a significant player among the urban centers of Eastern Europe.

---

[1] From time to time I will refer to Samuel as the "cultural informant."

On a national scale, Romania is a land in transition. Culturally, the region is a unique blend between Latin, Slavic, and Turkish elements, due to the multiple conquests by surrounding superpowers. Aioanei (2006) posits, "Romania's greatest historical curse is that it is settled in a land of inevitable domination and permanent interference of contradictory internationally political streams" (p.707). The southeast European region was ruled by various territorial rulers until the mid-nineteenth century, at which time a king was established as ruler of a united Romania. During the latter half of that century and the three decades of the twentieth, Romanian culture flourished. Consequently, nearly all of Romania's greatest cultural heroes lived during this period. Yet after the Second World War (1947), the Soviet-backed Communist Party held a tight control over the nation for well-over a generation, regulating every aspect of Romanians' lives from the types of food one may eat to how often one may take their car for a Sunday drive (Djuvara, 2014). Although the personal views of the cultural informant concerning this era will be offered in greater detail below, it is sufficient here to say that, for the vast majority of Romanians, life during the Communist period should never be relived again. As one Romanian historian writes, "The most tragic consequence of that half-century was that it destroyed our *soul*" (Djuvara, 2014, p. 342, emphasis his). Since 1989, the Romanian story is one of recuperation and slowly progressing to take its place in the industrialized world.

This year (2018) marks 29 years since the bloody Revolution of December 1989, meaning that a new generation has now matured that knows not firsthand the sting of Communism. But Samuel remembers. At 18 years old when the bullets started flying between the Communist secret police (Romanian: *Securitate*) and the Bucharest masses, Samuel had not only lived his entire childhood in Communist Romania but was also physically present during the protests that brought the socialist system crashing down. Samuel's is a unique story, as I have only met a small minority who grew up in Bucharest and are objective enough in the retelling to neither long for Romania's past nor berate their corrupt present. Because of his perspective as a true *Bucureştean,* I am confident that the picture he has painted of Romanian social organization is as authentic as possible.

On a day-to-day level, our cultural informant works as a shift manager at an electric company, where he has worked diligently since graduating from high school. Samuel, age 43, is happily married with three children, one from a former marriage and two young children at home. Although his wife is from a smaller city, Samuel and his family have only moved once (from the nearby apartment in which he was raised) and reside in a two-bedroom apartment near the southeast corner of Bucharest. It will soon become clear that it is Samuel's family, rather than his job title, of which he is most proud.

For Samuel in particular and for Romanians in general, the concepts of *kinship* and *family* are replete with both cultural and personal significance. In short, the family is the strongest network one can have, since it is usually through familial networks that basic needs are met. Studying the reciprocal nature of family and networks is the subject of the following section.

Networks and Control

When discussing how Romanians relate to one another socially, the importance of knowing terms for family members cannot be overstated. For this reason, I have listed these terms at the end of the chapter. According to the claims of Schusky (1983), kinship is one of the most central problems in the study of anthropology (p. 4). Again, in the opinion of this writer, the family is the most basic network from which Romanians tend to base their decisions. Theirs is a collectivist mentality that places more emphasis on group thinking than individual choice.

For Samuel, this is something he learned from his mother. Although his father was somewhat distant during his childhood, Samuel's mother was both his rock of support and the one in the family who could use their networks to meet needs. Recalls Samuel, "My mom was a secretary at the hospital, so we had some advantages in cases where we needed doctors or dentists. We didn't have to pay a bribe because it was much easier for us. It was a system where colleagues understood one another and would help each other." Evidently, such was life under the Communist regime, where one's networks stemmed primarily from family and friends who could be called upon at any time to reciprocate a favor.

When asked directly how Romanians define "family," Samuel responded in such a surprising fashion that it is worth quoting at length here:

> The purpose for which you live. The purpose for which you work. For us as Romanians, the family is an ideal, I can say. It cannot always be explained, meaning that at no time did I ever learn what 'family' actually means. It is a community of people who have the same interest even though they are different people, trying to find an equilibrium or balance to hold together a group and the interests of the group. Meaning that you develop and identify as a single group compared to the rest of the world as a family, as a name. For us as Romanians, family is very important, and this theme plays out in everything. So if you work, you work for the family. And if you do something extraordinary, you do it for the family. If you steal, because there are many people caught doing this, they declare that they did it for their family even if they have to sacrifice themselves.

6

> . . So it is a thing that for us as Romanians, family is everything.

From an anthropological viewpoint, these words of the cultural informant are immensely significant. Although he speaks in general terms, Samuel is claiming here that the family is the unit around which the Romanian's world revolves. From the cradle to the grave, families take care of each other.

At least three observations are noteworthy here as this study continues. First, a functional family that helps one another in all situations and celebrates each member's victories is the ideal. This cultural norm is displayed especially when it comes to hiring a "babysitter" for children; it is unthinkable for most Romanians to hire someone to daily watch their child when the grandparents live nearby. Second, everything one accomplishes in life reflects upon their family. The realization of goals is not as much personal as it is social. Finally, although blood relations form the strongest ties in Romanian families, a "family" can also be closely-knit as an interest group. Activities can be "helped along" by tight friendship networks, and generally close friends and office colleagues take no issue with helping one another out in small construction projects or even financial crises.

Anthropologist Lawrence Rosen (1984), in his examining of how Moroccans use networks to advance personal goals, maintains that network-driven cultures are in a constant state of negotiating how far one may push the relationship. Although his work refers specifically to Muslim contexts, his conclusions also ring true for the strong dependency upon family and friendship networks in Romania. These observations are critical to understanding Romanian kinship and family relations and will also serve a crucial role in the latter half of this study as possible ministry strategies are developed.

Interests and Ambitions

Dealing with interests and ambitions can be highly subjective but nevertheless is a discussion concerning the understanding of worldview and human nature of both the researcher and the researched. Redfield (1989) notes that how one understands human nature will affect how they order their social world (p. 48). As has already been shown, interests and ambition play key roles in how Romanian networks develop, allowing greater control to both physical and social resources. Further, Adams (1975) reminds that *power* refers to the ability of a person or group to coerce action, whereas *control* is a one-way action that cannot be reciprocated (pp. 21-24). Through the use of networks in Romanian society, power and control are a daily reality.

Samuel also sees the importance of interests, ambition, and controlling resources. Because his family is his most cherished resource, Samuel has little concern for excess *property* and *money* and hardly any concern at all for personal *prestige*. He does, however, believe that practical knowledge is the greatest resource a person may acquire. Likewise, it is praise from Samuel's family for his "handyman" housework, such as repairing his apartment's balcony siding, that means the most to him.

The cultural informant also recognizes that modern Romanians genuinely value education and advanced degrees. Samuel tells me that, during the Communist period, this was not the case. In fact, college-educated workers were often looked down upon as having "lost four or five years of working." Nowadays, however, many urban Romanians graduate from college and also decide to go further by earning a master's degree to bolster their CV for potential employment opportunities.

Although this researcher was surprised to find Samuel as an example of one who did not desire personal prestige, Romania is considered a "high power distance culture" (The Hofstede Center, 2014, http://geert-hofstede.com/united-states.html). Power distance refers to the degree to which individuals and organizations accept differences in status, particularly from the view point of lower status members (Hofstede et. al., 2010). High power distance cultures accept inequality as unavoidable fact, whereas low power distance cultures prefer egalitarianism (p. 61). This means that Romanians are generally comfortable with the fact of inequality among societal members. Special recognition is given to individuals who have attained higher education degrees, multiple titles and credentials, or elders. Although Samuel did return to the university to earn his master's degree in 2010, which he views as a necessity under the current system, he does not wish to flaunt his education level or feel the need to use it to seek better employment elsewhere.

To reiterate, the cultural informant's observations demonstrate that it is one's family and personal space that are of utmost importance to Romanians in general and *Bucureşteni* in particular. When asked where he feels the most at peace and if he has his own "personal space," Samuel emphatically gestures to his apartment and exclaims, "This is my personal space, from the door to the bathroom to the balcony, and it doesn't matter if Vlad [his five-year-old son] comes and I'm tired; it doesn't affect me. . . . Even if we are out on the street, my personal space is with my family." Indeed, the informant's two young children are at ages which demand more time at home than out in the city, but Samuel's words still exhibit deep attachment that is difficult to overstate. From childhood, Romanian children are taught that the bond between parent and child is the most intrinsic and long-lasting relationship of one's life. In contrast to American children, Samuel relates how Romanian children often sleep in the same bed as their parents until the age of three or four, whereby parents are nonverbally teaching their children that their parents will always be there if needed. Samuel continues, "But for us (as Romanians), we are very, very close to our children, almost exaggeratedly close, but this is how we feel. For me it seems very cold to leave the child to sleep by himself because he needs affection. For me the happiest child is in the mother's arms, because they need something to offer love and protection." Indeed, this custom sounds odd to American ears, where personal sleeping space is clearly structured for each family member.

Below is a basic schematic of Samuel's bloc apartment that he drew himself. Most Romanian apartments include a kitchen (*bucătărie*), living room (*sufragerie/camera de zi*), bathroom (*baie*), closet (*debara*), and often a balcony (*balcon*). Although their apartment has two bedrooms (*dormitor*), their family of four all sleeps in *Dormitor 1*. As mentioned above, because Samuel's two children are both young and his wife, Diana, remains home with them, this apartment forms the centerpiece of his world.

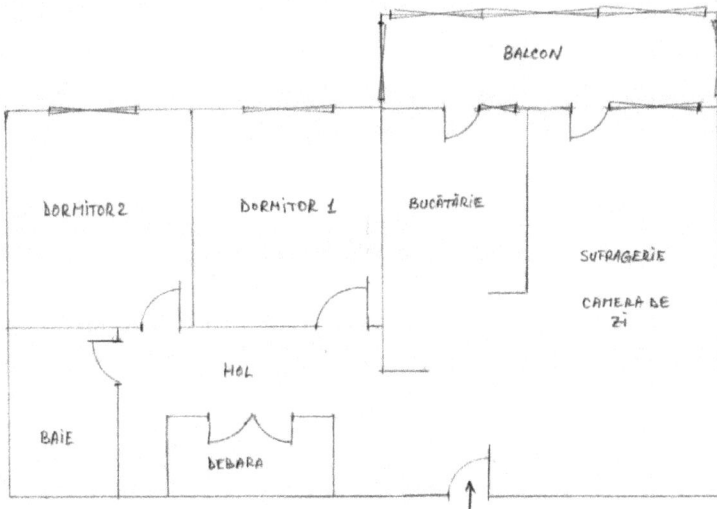

Redfield (1989) is again correct in arguing that, for urban dwellers, social organization is based on personal relationships more than individual roles within the community (p. 124). More stock is placed in people than in land and property, especially since living areas are small and the city of Bucharest is ever growing. As has been briefly shown from the life of our cultural informant Samuel, family and close friends form the basis of Romanian society.

Turning now to the development of ministry strategy, specifically aiming toward planting churches filled with people like Samuel, targeting the elements of *person-oriented relationships* and *family* must stand over and above a tendency toward *power* and *prestige*. In addition to the preceding themes being developed for practical purposes, the "Applications to Ministry" section will also take the form of an address to mission board leaders in church planting implementation in Bucharest. The study will then conclude by offering further research possibilities in the study of social anthropology and ministry in Bucharest, Romania.

Applications to Ministry

My colleagues and I serve with Team Bucharest and are committed to church planting in a city that is less than 1% evangelical. Although the map presented below is roughly ten years old and based solely on Baptist figures, it is indeed the southeast corner of the country (where Bucharest is located) that maintains

12

the lowest evangelical presence. The west and central regions of Romania, often called the "Bible Belt of Eastern Europe," consistently retain the highest percentage of evangelicals in the country.

Source: "Baptists from Romania (2002)",
http://commons.wikimedia.org/wiki/File:Baptisti_Romania_%282010
%29.png.

Our task is great and cannot be accomplished without a desperate reliance on God, because it is ultimately the Lord's work and not our own; and on an improved knowledge of Romanian culture, because it is with Romanian people that the work will be carried out. We need to understand not only the art of intercultural communication, but also let Romanians teach us how their society operates.

Over a period of several months, I have had the opportunity to interview a Romanian friend named

Samuel concerning these issues. This has been a wonderful experience for my wife and me to reach deeper into the lives of our Romanian friends. My purpose in writing is twofold. First, I will present to you my findings and explain how these ideas may help in further church planting efforts. Second, I will suggest further areas of exploration into understanding how the people of Bucharest may be impacted for Christ. It is my hope that, after reading this essay, we might all become excited to gather together better informed for brainstorming and strategizing sessions.

I will begin by explaining my research design. Veteran missiologists have long posited that cross cultural workers must gain an insider understanding of social structure, especially that of the family, to better grasp how worldview is shaped and changed in the host culture. Evangelism with the intention of church planting must target households, not simply individuals, and any attempts to engage cultural leaders should reflect established social structure lines. Apeh (1989) writes, "Leadership built along [existing] structures will help the nationals to relate to each other and to accept what is presented as a non-foreign package" (p. 87). The power of the gospel is most clearly on display when the hard work of critical contextualization has been done successfully, exhibited robustly in new groups and churches thriving in a biblical unity unique to their cultural setting.

Further, one may also draw upon the conclusions reached by Lingenfelter (1996), in which the missionary in intercultural contexts must be constantly seeking a deeper level of understanding of the social environment of those to whom he ministers. In *Transforming Culture,* Lingenfelter (1996) outlines five steps toward the comprehension of social environments: map the space, define the players, identify the primary relationships, explain essential activities, and identify the time and calendar of those activities (pp. 35-40). In my interviews with Samuel, the questions I generated were based heavily upon these five elements.

Having given a short introduction to the theory behind my desire to conduct these social organization interviews, I will now explain a bit more about the interview process and what I believe its strengths and weaknesses are for church planters. As mentioned above, Samuel graciously obliged to six interviews; each lasted roughly an hour and was conducted solely in the Romanian language. Although originally written in English, I translated my questions into Romanian and was afterward assisted by my language teacher (Samuel's wife) in crafting them in a more "Romanian-sounding" fashion. Each interview was built around a specific topic, such as personal interests or resources, and the questions were written in an open-ended method so that Samuel could elaborate as much as he wished. Not only was the information he provided fascinating, but through it all Samuel and I truly became friends as he also entrusted me with personal views on matters that clearly matter most to him.

Born and raised in the southern sector of Bucharest, Samuel was eighteen years old at the time of the Romanian Revolution in 1989. This means that his entire childhood was lived during the Communist period, and he vividly recalls standing in bread lines, playing with friends in empty parking lots, and parading through the neighborhood in his Communist *pionier* suit as an indoctrinated second grade student. Samuel personally stood alongside other young Romanians when the first shots rang out in late December 1989, signaling an end to the Communist regime. At 18, he went to work as an electrician, laboring hard and pulling odd shifts, and now at 43 he still works for the same company.

While nearly all Romanians I have spoken with have an opinion one way or the other, Samuel is refreshingly honest in saying that you cannot truly compare life before 1989 with life afterward. Both times have their problems, Samuel says, although nowadays Romanians have the opportunity to emigrate to Western Europe, the United States, or Canada. But Samuel and his wife are generally happy with their life in Bucharest, although they do wish that perhaps their two young children will find jobs in countries with higher GDPs than Romania. In order to further analyze the data, I have broken the subjects into the following categories: Family and Kinship; Community; Status, Role, and Division of Labor; and Religious Beliefs. Each subject will be examined in turn.

Family and Kinship

It is Samuel's family of which he is most proud, considering them his greatest success in life and the reason for which he works and lives. Although he had a loving mother and has recently grown close to his father, Samuel remembers his father being distant and has thus resolved to everyday be an example of love and kindness to his wife and children. Samuel's definition of family is illuminating in constructing a picture of his worldview, and even though the following quote is lengthy, it is deservedly so. Family, says Samuel, is:

> The purpose for which you live. The purpose for which you work. For us as Romanians, the family is an ideal, I can say. . . For us as Romanians, family is very important, and this theme plays out in everything. So if you work, you work for the family. And if you do something extraordinary, you do it for the family. If you steal, because there are many people caught doing this, they declare that they did it for their family even if they have to sacrifice themselves. . . So it is a thing that for us as Romanians, family is everything. I think I said it well that it is an ideal to have a perfect family, to develop well.

The importance of family to Romanians cannot be overstated. Whatever the decision made or success achieved, Romanians are always aware that, at some level, their family will be part of the process. Major decisions that affect only the individual are not part of the grid that makes up the Romanian worldview system.

I have included in this document a list of Romanian family/kinship terms and their definitions. Though not including a separate term for nearly every family member, as is common in other cultures (see Schusky, 1983), the Romanian language reserves several extra kinship terms that help explain just how large the "family" really is. For example, the terms *naş* and *fin* (godfather and godson) become part of a Romanian family via Christian Orthodox marriage or baptism, and although not specifically blood relatives, are responsible for spiritual teaching throughout the remainder of their lives. In addition, the *cuscru-cuscră* relationship is set apart for the parents-in-law of the bride and groom, being the familial term they render for one another. Although such terminology sounds strange to Western ears, the cross cultural observer begins to comprehend how much larger is a Romanian friend's family than originally expected.

Community

Because Romanians place such a high emphasis on personal connections and networking, community is also a central component in Romanian social structure. Indeed, community is an extension of family. Samuel has related several stories from both before and after the fall of Communism when one's community rises to the occasion and is a help in time of need. Whether the need is financial, agricultural, or physical, friends stand ready to help one another.

Certainly, tight-knit communal help can be used for both good and ill gain. As a positive example, this summer Samuel plans to build a fence around the house his wife inherited in a small village a few hours' drive from Bucharest. Samuel declares, "I have already written a list of people I can speak with about what day to come and help me, and they are friends that will come even if I don't pay. They will eat with you and sleep there; it is a good relationship we have. As a negative example, political corruption at all levels is rampant in Romania. Using their networks for political gain and personal development has caused bribery to be viewed as simply part of the culture.

Status, Role, and Division of Labor

The Hofstede Center reports that Romania is a "high power distance culture" (2015, http://geert-hofstede.com/romania.html). This means that the nation is quite comfortable viewing certain individuals as having greater prestige than others. In Romania, power distance and prestige are often awarded for advanced academic degrees, robust work experience, and age. Surprisingly, however, Samuel does not fit this mold. On the contrary, he has refused employment promotions that would offer greater prestige on more than one occasion. Although he is the shift manager, Samuel does not seek to rise higher in the ranks simply to build up his resume or so that others will be dependent on him. It is here that Samuel's humility and "family man" personality truly comes to be displayed, exclaiming, "For me, I go to work so that I can earn money! I don't go to work to become the boss or the director." To say the least, Samuel's attitude toward business and competition is refreshing, albeit not a full picture of Romanian workers.

Also within this category of status and role is the division between gender roles. Although traditional gender roles seem to be breaking down in the global West, Romania maintains a fairly sharp distinction. In the home, for example, women cook, clean, and give primary care to the children, whereas the husband works long hours for a generally miniscule salary (as compared with other countries). In Bucharest, however, wives will often work in order to assist with the high costs of renting or owning an apartment. This is not always true, of course, as seen in the case of Samuel's family. During the language classes my wife and I take from Samuel's wife in their apartment, for example, Samuel happily watches their kids and does the household chores like laundry and dishes. Still, it is important to recall that men and women in Romania often retain such a strict gender role division.

Religious Beliefs

According to the National Institute of Statistics Romania (2013), 86% of Romanians are Eastern Orthodox. To be Romanian, it is said, is to be Orthodox, and therefore it is no surprise that Samuel and his family are Orthodox. At the conclusion of our six interviews, Samuel was thoroughly generous in also answering my questions concerning his opinion of the state of Orthodoxy in Romania. He addressed multiple topics, including how it is passed on from one generation to the next, Romanians' receptivity to new religious ideas, and which family member is responsible for leading the family in spiritual matters.

Although he agrees that most Romanians are not "practicing" (and Romanian men are even less so), Samuel believes that it is the parents' responsibility to impart religious teaching to their children. Though Samuel would not consider himself a much of a "practicing" Orthodox, his wife occasionally teaches their children about the Bible and how to say the more well-known prayers like "Our Father." If the parents are not religious, he believes, the children are much less likely to choose to practice religion. In Samuel's words, "Maybe when you are young you don't want to have anything to do with religion and you do many things on your own power, but when you get older you start to have fear about what will happen after death and you know how many sins you made in your life and probably this desire appears to become closer to God, a relationship, you might say, that will last further." There is, then, always a possibility of seeking after God, be it based on parental guidance or the fear of mortality.

When it comes to religion, Samuel believes the most significant element is that it should not be forced on anyone. Being an educated man, Samuel believes that new ideas should be presented and everyone allowed their own opinion. In fact, he even goes so far as to say that "parents are morally obligated to pass along this faith and to take the child to church and to talk about God and to read the stories," because doing so offers the child a state of moral balance that can only assist them in the future. Samuel is fully aware that children must be equipped to respond to basic worldview questions such as "why was I born?" and "what should I do with my life?" In short, religious beliefs are a necessary and welcome reality that should be allowed in the realms of society and family.

Conclusion

The preceding analysis of Romanian social organization is significant for future church planting strategy, particularly as it relates to Bucharest, in at least three ways: evangelism via family and community networks, evangelism that recognizes the importance of the home, and evangelism that emphasizes openness to new ideas over force and coercion. First, this study has sought to demonstrate the strength of Romanian family and community relationships. As has been mentioned more than once, the emphasis Romanians place upon family and friendships cannot be driven far enough. For Samuel, the cultural informant, family is so significant that he has turned down advancement in employment and opportunities to seek jobs in other cities and countries because his chief concern is providing a quality life for his family. Evangelists and church planters, likewise, cannot afford to overlook how Romanians faced with the prospect of conversion from Orthodoxy to evangelicalism will be viewed by their families. As evangelists and church planters, we must ask the difficult questions concerning the social and economic shame that conversion could bring to a Romanian with an Orthodox family background. It is therefore encouraged that any evangelism done among Romanians also have a plan in place for reaching one's entire family and personal networks, either through group Bible studies or training new converts to use these networks for the spread of God's Kingdom.

Second, evangelistic outreach must recognize the importance of the home. As written above, because it is where his wife and children spend most of their time, Samuel's apartment forms the central arena of his world. Not only so, but it is also one of the things in Samuel's life for which he is proud, often hosting neighbors and family members for parties and cookouts. Bible studies conducted in apartments, while not at all the norm for Romanian Orthodox people, may encourage Romanian families to see firsthand how the Bible is meant to affect normal everyday life. Of course, many Romanian apartments are not large, but outgrowing one's living room because there are too many people interested in Bible study is perhaps the best problem one could have.

Third, evangelism and church planting in Romania should emphasize openness instead of force or coercion. In general, Romanians are tired of having religious teaching forced upon them by their elders and priests. Nevertheless, I have also heard many Romanians declare in frustration that the Bible is too difficult to understand on one's own, thus perpetuating the idea that only priests can explain spiritual things. This is not the case. All Christians should be willing and able to teach biblical truth and explain it (Matthew 28:19-20). Obedience in evangelism must be taught in both Romanian evangelical churches and missionary circles, especially those methods that winsomely call for a response in repentance and discipleship.

More work is needed in the realm of social anthropology and missiology in a Romanian context. From a research standpoint, little missiological work has been done that seeks to utilize Romanian opinions about the inner-workings of their culture and how the gospel affects family and kinship networks. From a practical ministry standpoint, Romanian evangelicalism looks and sounds nearly identical to American evangelicalism, almost always making the Romanian Orthodox instantly uncomfortable upon entering a foreign, evangelical church. Lingenfelter (1996) wisely reminds readers that every culture's social structure is a reality that presents both good and bad, but for the Christian there is a divine, "pilgrim alternative" wherein he or she finds a home in "sustained nonconformity" (p. 232). Living in and understanding Romanian social structure while simultaneously confronting its woes is a high calling for the cross cultural worker, but still they can rest assured that the One who calls is faithful.

Cameron D. Armstrong

Romanian Kinship Terms

mamă	mother
tată	father
frate	brother
soră	sister
nepot	nephew/grandson
nepoată	niece/granddaughter
bunic	grandfather
bunică	grandmother
străbunic	great-grandfather
străbunică	great-grandmother
cumnat	brother-in-law
cumnată	sister-in-law
mătuşă	aunt
unchi	uncle
naş	godfather (by baptism or marriage)
naşă	godmother (by baptism or marriage)
fin	godson (by baptism or marriage)
fină	goddaughter (by baptism or marriage)
văr, verişor	male cousin
vară, verişoară	female cousin
cuscru	father of son/daughter-in-law
cuscră	mother of son/daughter-in-law
socru	father-in-law
soacră	mother-in-law
noră	daughter-in-law
ginere	son-in-law
-vitreg(ă)	all family members who are not blood relatives (half-sister/brother, step-sister/brother, etc.)

CHAPTER TWO:

LEADERSHIP PATTERNS IN ROMANIA AND
FUTURE MISSIOLOGICAL IMPLICATIONS

In terms of leadership, Romania is a rapidly evolving nation. Since the Revolution in 1989, Romania has crept closer each year to the leadership models exhibited by its Western influencers. Yet Romania retains one firmly planted foot in the older pattern of highly centralized leadership. Due to its burgeoning status as an international voice, however, the nation also ventures cautiously forward with the other foot toward a more progressive and democratic leadership style. This blend of "old and new world" mentalities presents a unique opportunity for students of leadership and management theory to identify and engage such challenges arising in the Romanian leadership landscape. The study will demonstrate a firmly-rooted system of autocratic leadership that is a holdover from Communist days, while at the same time yielding a blossoming desire for individual autonomy that is only in its beginning stages.

In what follows, I will attempt to delineate current leadership patterns in the country of Romania. Personal experience, interpersonal testimony, and published materials allow Romanian culture to be examined and primary models to be identified; this is done with regard to leadership at both the local and national levels. Afterward, I will offer several implications for missionary strategy, including church planting efforts, developing and raising up disciples, and general mission education.

Defining Leadership

Leadership is the study of leaders and how they influence others. In her study entitled "Leadership in Romania," Aioanei (2006) defines a leader and leadership in the following manner:

> The leader is a person who occupies a position of responsibility in coordinating the activities of group members in their task of attaining a common goal. Leaders must mobilize their constituents to do something, and induce their willingness to do it. Leaders are those who give credibility to their words by their actions. Leadership is not only about leaders but also about followers. Followers are the mechanism through which common goals are achieved. An adequate analysis of leadership also involves situations; conditions under which leader behaviors are effective (p. 706).

Leaders, then, are both coordinators working from the top-down and mobilizers working from within in order to effect change and the realization of goals. This model is helpful in understanding the diversity of leadership, noting that leaders' credibility is also based on followers' responses and the situation-specific realities in which the multiple players interact.

Also important for the following study on Romanian leadership is the "four frames" model set forth by Bolman and Deal (2003). The four frames are structural (companies are composed like a factory), human resource (extended family), political (competitive arena), and symbolic (theater). In this pivotal analysis, Bolman and Deal explain that executives tend to lead from a single frame that inhibits their ability to respond to conflict and change in the workplace. While each frame retains its usefulness, the authors advocate that leaders utilize all four frames when possible. As will be shown below, Romanian leaders at nearly every level manage almost exclusively along the structural and political frames. First, however, I will explain some of the cultural history of Romania.

Romanian Leadership Patterns

Nestled against the Black Sea, the country of Romania is the only Latin-based culture in Eastern Europe. Romanians are proud of their history, even though it has regularly consisted of foreign powers conquering their lands. Because of Romania's location and turbulent past, there is a unique mixture of Turkish, Russian, Slavic, German, and most recently, Western influences. Aioanei (2006) posits, "Romania's greatest historical curse is that it is settled in a land of inevitable domination and permanent interference of contradictory internationally political streams" (p.707). Until the Communist advance following World War II, unified Romania was a monarchy (Djuvara, 2014).

Romania is nearly 30 years removed from the bloody revolution of December 1989, the nation-wide conflict which concluded after the Communist leader-dictator, Nicolae Ceausescu, and his wife were captured and executed. After over 60 years of hardline socialism, Romania began their uphill struggle toward democracy. Immediately the former Communist Party leaders took over, and, although free elections were held since 1991, post-communist Romania has consistently elected national leaders who served in moderate to high leadership roles in the Communist party prior to 1989.

Although modern Romania, especially its larger cities, is characterized by a fervent openness to the West, the culture retains its idea that the best way for leaders to execute tasks is through a centralized, authoritative figure. Individual leaders providing stricter project boundaries, it is assumed, will yield the most effective results and security (Aioanei, 2006, p. 708). Such reasoning is indeed a byproduct from monarchic and Communist times, but may also be due to several other factors.

In their fascinating "Age cohort effects, gender, and Romanian leadership preferences" by Fein, Tziner, and Vasiliu (2010), the hypothesis was tested that

Romanian managers under the age of 35 are more apt to exhibit a more Western-style, individualistic behavior that focuses more on the workers' needs than on workers' tasks. After surveying 324 male and female Romanian business managers, the researchers concluded that actually the younger managers are more prone toward autocratic, task-oriented values than those managers over 35 who had worked during Communism (pp. 372-373). Since 1989, Romania has continually completed each fiscal year in economic decline, and Romania's "best and brightest" often emigrate to the West. Thus there seems to be a pressure that younger Romanian executives feel if there is ever to be a way forward for their nation's economy.

Unfortunately, retaining a single Romanian leader who personally holds all the keys to centralized power creates a system ripe for corruption. Political scientists remind us that it is impossible to study leadership without also analyzing power. Adams (1975) writes, "Power is ...derived from relative control by each actor or unit over elements of the environment of concern to the participants" (pp. 9-10). Power deals with one's coercive influence over the energies of others. Yet, whereas *power* concerns both the leader and the follower, *control* is a forceful, one-way relationship that cannot be reciprocated (Adams, 1975, pp. 21-24). In a Romanian setting, this reality of power and control is showcased daily in a variety of arenas.

One such example of the use and abuse of power and control among Romania's leadership involves the redistribution of vast tracts of Romania's "public lands" after the fall of Communism. Verdery (2002) notes that the Romanian government passed a law in 1991 to redistribute all public tracts of land (such as forests and farms) that were collectivized in 1959 (pp. 9). The plan was to commission local agents to survey and restore ownership rights to villagers who could offer "genuine proof" that the lands belonged to their families before 1959. In effect, this act legally concentrated a single resource which everyone desired in the hands of teams of three committee members. Verdery (2002) offers the case of one Mayor Lupu of Hunedoara County, who for almost a decade gave valuable lands to his allies and consistently blocked a legitimate heir of one of his property holdings from reclaiming her family's lands, without any fear of sanctions. Among other illegal measures, Mayor Lupu refused to stamp the heir's documents, postponed the official surveying of land for two years by requiring the heir to obtain documents in the capitol of Bucharest, and in the meantime the mayor lived on the land himself (pp. 12-16). In a similar case, Sikor, Stahl, & Dorondel (2008) detail the coercive tendencies of the mayor of the small village of Dragova in Romania's Transylvania region. The mayor, who is married to the owner of the village's logging company, gave unrestricted logging rights for the nearby public forests to his wife's company by manipulating the land commission to shrink personal property holdings. The mayor of Dragova evidently had many powerful friends in Parliament, giving the villagers the impression that, "if you fight with him, you fight with the state" (pp. 19-20). Using tactics like these to secure alliances based on scarce resources such as public lands, corrupt Romanian mayors and other political leaders are often reelected many times over.

Bribery, land-grabbing, and corruption are seen as structural products of the centralized power structure of Romania. In his excellent chapter called "Institution development and corruption in local society in southeastern Europe," Șerban (2007) believes that local Romanians do not have a specific definition of corruption and thus do not realize they are bribing officials (pp. 177). While corruption does exist throughout Romania, Șerban advances that certain areas, such as the western Banat region, resist corruption on a larger scale than other regions, such as Bucharest (pp. 180). A thorough study of leadership in Romania, then, must analyze the topic from the lens of particular regions under consideration. Also, a second lens that Șerban suggests for understanding Romanian leadership is what he labels "rurbanization," which is the interplay of cultural habits between villagers forced to move into cities during Communism and city-dwellers who have since moved back to their villages (pp. 180-181). Local leaders' degree of "rurbanization," especially degrees of literacy and history of business and political engagement, will undoubtedly affect leadership regime.

With these theories and experiences in mind, it is now possible to construct a model of Romanian leadership as it currently exists. Using the thoughts put forward by several Romanian management scholars, I will explain the concept of a centralized executive in terms of formally defined authority and unified group identity. I will then conclude this section by explaining how I believe the current Romanian leadership model is evolving.

Grid and Group

In his book *Transforming Culture,* author Sherwood Lingenfelter (1998) follows other cultural anthropologists in identifying social orders with the terms *grid* and *group* (p. 102). Lingenfelter writes:

> We use grid to describe the different ways in which people define the place and role of individuals in a game or a social activity . . . We use group to describe the different ways in which people define the identity and relationships of members of a team, extended family, or community (pp. 26-27).

Grid, then, refers to how clearly social roles are defined. Group explains how great the members' sense of identity as unit is. "Strong grid" cultures depend heavily on specific, well-defined leaders. "Strong group" cultures, likewise, depend heavily on the unity and common bond of all group members. These helpful concepts can be used in better grasping Romanian leadership patterns.

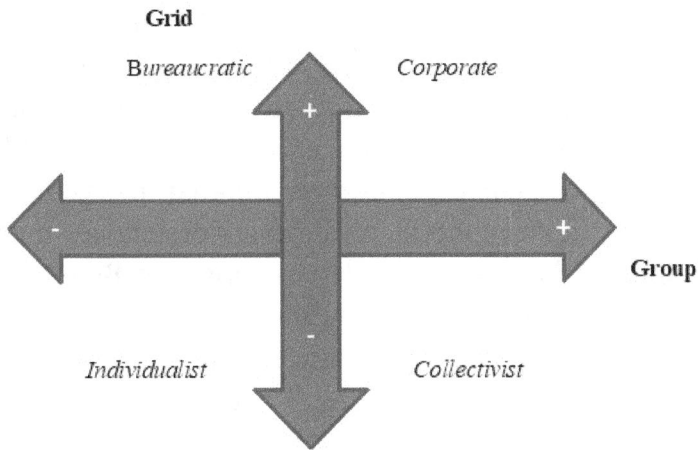

Grid

Bureaucratic   *Corporate*

Individualist   *Collectivist*

Group

By nature, Romania is a "strong *grid*" culture, although the younger generations are slowly moving down the scale. As a whole, though, responses and reactions are most often generated in formal settings by those Romanians holding the highest titles and earned degrees *ad nauseum*. When entering a business meeting, there is a clear pecking order where everyone knows who is in charge. Often such a group would be distinguished by the leader moving the conversation along by doing most of the talking. For example, when my wife and I attended our first Romanian wedding, we were seated next to the assistant pastor of our church.

Although our assistant pastor was simply a guest like the rest of us sitting around the table, it was his recognized role to begin and move along whatever we were discussing.

This social distinction is further reinforced through the Romanian language, which maintains a formal and informal way of addressing others. Whereas a Romanian will use informal forms of verbs speaking with friends and people younger than himself, the formal forms are always used with older people and men and women holding positions of authority in that context. As another personal example, I taught a class at the Baptist seminary in Bucharest, and, due to some students who were unable to speak English, I taught in Romanian. Because several of the students were older than me, I used the formal verb forms when speaking directly to them. Obviously surprised, these same students insisted on using the formal forms when addressing me. I realized later that it was because of my role as professor, even if only for the day and even if I was younger than they, which merited a "strong grid" mentality.[2]

Published leadership research supports these personal findings. Aioanei (2006) and a team of researchers distributed a survey to 100 highly educated

---

[2]This concept of using the Romanian formal verb forms seems to be somewhat region-specific, as well. In the extreme western part of the country, namely Timisoara and other cities with a strong Western influence, there appears less of an emphasis on linguistic formality in context.

Romanian business people and asked them to respond to several "leader-follower scenarios" to determine Romanians' desires for ideal leaders. Several of the survey's conclusions were expected, such as managers generally choosing not to involve subordinates in the decision-making process and handling projects in a task-before-people method. Although a decisive majority of the respondents favored authoritarian tactics in business management, 45% prefer more democratic leadership styles (p. 710). Aioanei concludes by observing that, although the data does indicate that preferences for participative leadership are growing year by year, the Romanian culture is not yet ready for a formal switch from an autocratic boss who will make all the real decisions to a collegial superior who will lead through negotiation and democracy (p. 711).

Unlike grid, Romanian *group* identity is not as easily definable. On the local level, Romanians hold tightly to their commitment to familial relationships and are usually not ashamed to explain in detail about the environment in which they were raised. Except for education and employment reasons, Romanians do not seriously consider moving to another city where they will not have any family connections. On the state level, Romanians' mistrust of political leaders stems from communist years and attempts to rally whole communities together to form cohesive groups is difficult. Constantin, Pop, and Stoica-Constantin (2006) contend that team-building strategies in the

Romanian workplace are quite rare, and thus are viewed by employers as insignificant issues dwarfed by a company's financial challenges ("Romanian managers and human resource management," p. 761).

Due to Western influence, the internet, English television programs, and a lengthening distance from their Communist past, Romanians are becoming increasingly aware of different leadership forms and styles. Younger Romanians especially, lacking firsthand experience under Communist rule, favor individualistic models and thus do not understand the higher degree of group-centered mentality indicative of older generations. Younger Romanians feel little patriotism, are disenchanted with Romanian culture, and often cannot wait to study or even move abroad; this "weak group" identity is only growing. Even so, it is the elder generation that currently retains the positions of authority in Romanian society, and this fact leads to the conclusion that the greatest group divisions in Romanian culture are between the old and younger generations. Until another post-Communist generation matures, this age divide may prove the greatest challenge in genuinely uniting the Romanian people.

In Lingenfelter's (1998) terms, Romanian status quo remains fixed in a *Bureaucratic* social game, based on strong grid and weak group identity, but the upcoming generations are gradually shifting toward an *Individualist* construct, based on weak grid and weak group identity (*Transforming culture,* p. 31). As power is slowly wrested from the autocratic to the democratic, Romanian leaders will continue to debate the most effective methods of impacting their people. Indeed, consistent oscillation between centralized and coordinated units of power is expected in political theory (Adams, 1975, p. 300). What is and will continue to challenge Christian missionaries is how to utilize the preceding observations regarding Romanian leadership patterns to also generate the greatest possible impact. Although the impact missionaries intend to have is for the cause of Christ, instead of the accumulation of personal power, it is to this end that this study now turns.

Missiological Implications

To begin, I will first explain my role as a missionary. My wife and I, since our appointment six years ago, serve in Bucharest. At base we are church planters, laboring to form small groups of Romanians interested in studying the Bible that will eventually transition into New Testament churches.[3] Our sending organization is the International Mission Board (IMB) of the Southern Baptist Convention. The IMB has had a presence in Romania for nearly 100 years, although mission work

---

[3] As Baptist missionaries, we define a "New Testament church" as a local, covenanted group of baptized believers that regularly practice baptism, the Lord's Supper, worship, biblical teaching, and evangelistic activity (Hammett, 2005). Baptist work will receive specific attention in this paper.

inside the country was severely limited during World War II and the Communist period.

Church planting in the Bucharest area is progressing, albeit slower than other regions of the country. The western and central regions of Romania, considered informally as the "Bible Belt of Eastern Europe," contain the largest evangelical presence in Romania, whereas the southern and eastern regions, where Bucharest is located, retain an evangelical presence of less than 1%. According to map below, although based solely on Baptist figures, it is indeed the southern and eastern segments of the country where future church planting efforts must be catalyzed.

Several Romanian churches have caught the vision for multiplication and others are interested in attempting new strategies to reach the shifting culture of Bucharest. Pastor Cornel, a former president of the Bucharest Baptist Association, believes that the primary reason he was elected to lead the association is because of his dedication to the relatively new discussion on church planting. If Cornel is correct, therefore, there is a growing desire among the leaders of the Bucharest Baptist Association for more churches to be planted in the city and in its surrounding territory.

Source: "Baptists from Romania (2002)",
http://commons.wikimedia.org/wiki/File:Baptisti_Romania_%
282010%29.png.

Such healthy discussions signal several promising factors, of which missionaries of all stripes must take note and encourage. First, Romanian Baptists are beginning to think differently in terms of outreach strategy and what that might look like for the map above to turn a shade darker. Second, there are some pastors, especially younger ones, who are beginning to experiment with small group methodology that pushes against the ecclesiastical status quo. Third, missional identity at the member level, based on the crucial doctrine of the priesthood of the believer, is beginning to be discussed among younger pastors across denominational lines. I will briefly explain each of these elements below.

1. Thinking Differently. In an interview with Bucharest Baptist Association leader and past president, whom I will simply call Cornel, confided that,

> Long ago we would host evangelistic meetings, and many people would be curious and come, but that does not work now, **and is not efficient.** Two years ago we started using a tent for outdoor meetings, but now we've stopped that. Just a few months ago I **began to stress biblical discipleship** – small group Bible study meetings like Jesus did.

Urban mission work must, by nature, shift with the times. For Cornel, "small groups like Jesus did" has become his new go-to model for evangelistic outreach, not because it is easier than tent meetings but because of the emphasis on deeper discipleship that will outlast the event.

2. *Small Groups.* Whereas Cornel's church is now on the cusp of small group experimentation, Bucharest does have a few young evangelical churches that have pursued small groups as part of their DNA. It would be wise for future missionary endeavors to partner with these creative pastors who are willing to "think outside the box." Personally, I am aware of ten churches, Baptist and Brethren, in Bucharest proper that were planted with this strategy. The small group model is new to Romanian culture, which emphasizes individual leader empowerment that is detached from the head pastor; it seems that only in those churches

with a majority of younger members is the model working in terms of numerical growth. I will speak more to this concept in a moment.

3. Missional Identity. Over the last several years, Romanian pastors and leaders from some of Bucharest's most strategically innovative churches meet periodically for mutual encouragement in the constant pursuit of fresh ways to engage the city. I have attended two of their gatherings, and it is exciting to watch Romanians taking ideas from missional thinkers in other parts of the globe and asking how that might look in a Bucharest context. This interdenominational group is small and is made up of perhaps ten churches, at the most, and none of the city's larger evangelical churches are represented.

These three characteristics demonstrate a growing desire among Bucharest's evangelical churches, specifically among the Baptists and Brethren, for church structure and strategy to adapt with the times. Yet a genuine warning of caution must be upheld when advocating rapid change, and, of course, all things must be filtered biblically. Conspicuously absent from the discussions I have attended is a common wrestling with biblical texts *before* wrestling with missiological models and buzzwords. It is my conclusion, therefore, that, while such fresh efforts for Romanians reaching the city are healthy, missionaries may still play a key role in advancing kingdom efforts through reproducible methods that clearly hail directly from the Scriptures and move Christians to engage the lost world around them. As I see it, the modern missionary's role in Bucharest is to be a living example of authentic dependence and heartfelt obedience to God's Word, proven by their witness as biblically-centered disciples who unashamedly take risks to ensure that the church leaders they mentor and/or work with are never satisfied with status quo ministry.[4] To that end, I have worked closely with my team leader to attempt to articulate further missionary goals and outreach strategy in Bucharest.

Using the conclusions supplied in the earlier section of this analysis that Romanian leadership tends toward a bureaucratic scenario, I offer the following diagrams as ministry models. The first diagram depicts current trends in Romanian churches, and the second diagram reflects a possible structure for what we believe will be biblically-sound Romanian church plants. Each diagram will be briefly discussed.

Diagram 1. Average Romanian Baptist church model.

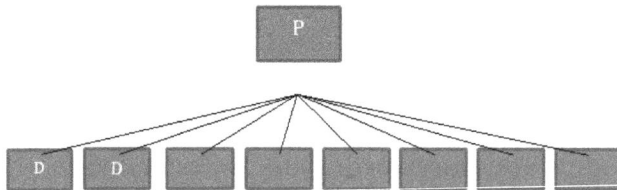

[4]Indeed, this concept of the role of the missionary should hold true in all fields with established churches, structures, unions, etc.

The first diagram represents the average Romanian Baptist church, which usually employs one or perhaps two pastors (P) and one or two unpaid deacons (D) serve in various administrative roles. As is indicated, the pastor is clearly in control; all ministry decisions flow from him to the people. There is little room for individuality among church members and hardly any accountability for the pastor. As such, whenever individual members do have outreach ideas, the pastor must openly approve them, and he must take the initiative in leading.

This is a single leader model that often assumes that the pastor can be the only leader (except perhaps sometimes the church's deacons), the only one in the church to train and disciple others, and the only one in the church to conduct outreach. As these responsibilities prove too much for any one person, Romanian Baptist pastors are generally exhausted men who truly believe it is their call from God to do all these things. Because the pastor can only do so much, life-on-life discipleship that could be done from one member to another suffers. While this church model does meet the Romanian "high grid" desire for structure and knowing precisely who is in charge (Aioanei, 2006, p. 708), it also exhibits "low group" trends by not empowering church members to become commonly united (Constantin, Pop, & Stoica-Constantin, 2006, p. 761).

All this is not to say that Romanian churches with single elder models cannot be healthy and effective. Without providing an all-out defense of the single leader model, a few remarks must be noted. Pastors *should* be recognized and obeyed as the church's rightful leaders (Heb. 13:17; 1 Tim. 5:17). Pastors *should* be honored and followed based on their qualifications as leaders and blameless conduct (1 Tim. 3:1-7; Tit. 1:5-9). Pastors *should* be held in esteem for their aptness in rightly teaching God's Word from the pulpit as a preacher and in the outside-the-church gathering as an evangelist (Tit. 1:9; 2 Tim. 4:2, 5).

On the other hand, there are at least two inherent downfalls in a church model that holds the pastor as the only real leader, with one coming from the part of the pastor and the other coming from the role of the member. First, pastors who serve as the only leader may be tempted to rule the church as an unchecked CEO (Hammett, 2005, p. 153). Such temptations arise due to lack of accountability, which may or may not be provided by pastors of other churches that congregants know nothing about. Second, church members may be tempted to forgo their own Christian duties of service to their church and evangelistic outreach. When a single pastor is tasked with motivating and discipling everyone, individual Christians may falsely consider their place as "lowly church member" to be unimportant in the eyes of God.

Diagram 2. Small group-based church multiplication model.

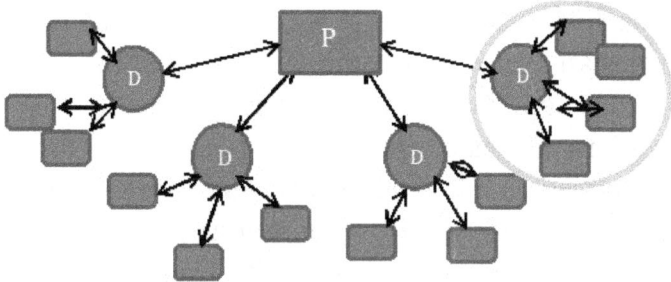

I have labeled this second model the small group-based church multiplication model. As shown in Diagram 2 above, the pastor (P) is closely connected to the small group leaders, who also serve as deacons (D) in that they assist the pastoral team in service and outreach (Acts 6:1-7). Their relationship rises and falls with close accountability and discipleship between all parties, denoted by the arrows advancing in both directions. With multiplication as the stated goal, small groups should be ready to break up and form new groups when they reach a large enough size. This size limit is determined by several factors, including pastoral advice, spatial context, and overall group hegemony. Further, after a small group reproduces itself several times, pastors by that point must be willing for small group networks to form their own reproducing church. In this case, the deacon (D) will transition to the role of pastor (P), and the process starts again.

Again, this second method rises and falls on accountability and discipleship between the pastor and the small group leaders/deacons (Heb. 10:24-25). Because of Romanians' high grid reliance on specific titles and roles that come directly from the leader, it is recommended that the pastor meet with small group leaders at least once every two weeks for mutual encouragement, discipleship, and theological training. Likewise, any second generation small group leaders should also meet regularly with the leader of the first generation group plant, and so on. It is essential that every church member can clearly trace their small group leader's power back to the church's pastor. Habitual and honest communication between the pastor and church leaders should ensure sound teaching that each small group member knows, beyond a shadow of a doubt, their pastor is aware and approves of group methods. In addition, pastors utilizing the small group-based multiplication strategy are advised to personally visit individual small groups once per quarter in order to provide visible justification that the church's primary leader approves of the group.

Transitioning a Romanian evangelical church, especially a traditional one, to the second model will not be easy and will take many years. Even younger churches like the one I attend, whose vision falls quite close to this, are largely filled with Romanian believers who have grown up in traditional-style churches. It is at this particular juncture where I view the foreign evangelical missionary to be the most effective. There are at least five areas to be highlighted, each element building on the last. (1) Missionaries must mentor pastors in releasing control of personally leading every gathering, however large. Nowhere in the world is the release of pastoral control not a controversial issue, and this is exhibited in the high grid culture of Romania, as well. (2) Missionaries must model small group discussion methods where the leader is not the single speaker. Pastors and small group leaders are often talented preachers, but there should be general recognition that the small group is meant to enhance individual discipleship and is neither the time nor the place for sermons. (3) Missionaries must take evangelism and discipleship seriously by advocating that their disciples make disciples. The most effective model of this type of discipleship is, of course, the Lord Jesus, who took his disciples with him to evangelize and then sent them out to do the same. (4) Missionaries must remember that the tools they use in Bible study must be simple enough to be replicated many times over by Christians who are not seminary-trained and do not possess multiple hours designated for personal study. Simplification will lead to multiplication. Small group members must see that their leader is teaching material from the Bible, so that when times are dark and the small group member is alone, they can know it is to God's Word, not a commentary, to which they must run. (5) Missionaries must daily demonstrate a deep commitment to the power of prayer and individual communion with the Lord. Small group members will respond to and begin to display in their own life, whether negatively or positively, the level of spiritual need expressed by their group leader.

Until church members personally catch the vision, small groups will remain *small* groups. The conclusion reached above concerning Romanian group identity is largely a *weak group* social game, where Romanians appreciate the freedom to opt out of group meetings. But this does not mean that small group leaders should be discouraged or that the model should be thrown out, because it is a biblical model based on mutual accountability, encouragement, and discipleship (Acts 2:46; Heb. 10:24-25). We must remember that God gives the growth, that He is always at work, and if He chooses to grow our number then it is for His glory, not ours (1 Cor. 3:7). At the same time, though, pastors and leaders of small group-based churches must be ever recasting the vision and reminding church members that small group attendance is *not* an "above and beyond" option but is essential as a member. But even if small groups hover for a time as *small groups* that are few in number, there is still little to fear and much to be commended. Families happily gathered together in a home environment, praying for one another, speaking truth to one another, and holding one another accountable as obedient disciples beautifully pictures practical Christianity that will soon cause neighbors to become curious and perhaps even join in.

Conclusion

Lingenfelter (1998) poignantly asserts that culture is not neutral, but is instead a "prison of disobedience" that Christians are to assist others in escaping from, pursuing instead the "pilgrim principle" (pp. 15-16). The "pilgrim principle" is based on biblical contextualization and a social game that moves toward the center of the grid and group graph, meaning that Christians should strive neither to remove themselves from culture nor remain fixated in any one of the four quadrants (p. 174). The pilgrim must travel a higher road: the "way of the cross" (p. 172).

For the foreign missionary, such words profoundly hit home. The stress of waking each morning in the midst of a culture whose social game regarding leadership is unfamiliar is disconcerting. Specifically, Romania is a *high grid* culture that values defined superiority in a way that I will never fully comprehend. Romania is also a *weak group* culture that by nature cares little about common group identity and prefers instead freedom from personal obligation.[5] These cultural and leadership tendencies are not those of Western cross-cultural missionaries like myself, thus making discomfort the rule rather than the

---

[5]With this being said, however, a positive pinpoint of high grid and low group will vary based on context. Age distinctions (old vs. young), local environment (city vs. village), and religious ties (Orthodox vs. evangelical) will inevitably nuance these findings.

exception. Pilgrims, however, are not at home in either Romanian or Western culture.

The missionary task in Romania is, of course, the same as anywhere else in the world. With faces set toward the divine task of making disciples who make disciples, missionaries must work with church leaders to ignite their dreams of a nation of vibrant, Spirit-filled Christians. A short survey of Romanian Baptist practices reveals that the traditional Romanian Baptist church is modeled after a single leader who is often overwhelmed with his multiple tasks and multiple disciples. The model suggested in this paper moves toward an ecclesiastical scheme based on individual accountability, discipleship, small group leader empowerment, and a deliberate breaking away of small group networks to form new, autonomous churches.

The century-long history of American missionary work with Romanian Baptists is one of both joy and sorrow – joy displayed by the many lasting partnerships and ministries started and sorrow exhibited in the murky depths of dependency on Western monies poured in after the fall of Communism. A genuine understanding of Romanian leadership patterns may form the crux of new discussions concerning the future of the missionary task in Romania. To that end, this investigation is offered.

CHAPTER THREE:

ROMANIAN-AMERICAN IDENTITY
NEGOTIATION:

A CASE STUDY IN INTERCULTURAL
COMMUNICATION

Since the fall of Communism in 1989, Romanians have struggled with the concept of identity on both a personal and national level. The opening of the Eastern European nation to the global West is nearly universally viewed in welcoming terms, especially among younger Romanians who did not mature under the Communist regime. Yet such a rapid cultural shift invariably involves the formation of a new cultural identity, an awareness that is keenly treated in intercultural communication terminology as "identity negotiation" (Ting-Toomey, 2005). As an American evangelical missionary working in Romania, I have noticed how Romanians who have spent extensive time with Americans "negotiate" a third type of identity. This fascinating reality, which I will label "Romanian-American," can best be understood in the analysis of a conversation between a Romanian friend named Adrian and myself.

In what follows, I will first explain the theory of identity negotiation, dipping also into the theory of intercultural accommodation. Several thoughts

53

concerning Romanian value orientations will then be offered. Finally, the discussion will transition to an analysis of how my friend Adrian uses communication techniques to negotiate a new identity.

Identity Negotiation Theory

Ting-Toomey (2005) defines identity as one's "reflective self-conception or self-image" (p. 212). Based largely on the values acquired in the home, especially in the early years, individuals develop a personal picture of how precisely males and females in their culture are supposed to think and act. Using an example from American culture, newborn baby boys are often wrapped in the hospital's blue blankets directly after birth, reiterating the idea that blue is a "boy color." Newborn girls, however, are often wrapped in pink blankets. Several years ago, when my brother decided to wear a pink shirt to school, my family and friends bristled at his move against societal norms. Identity crises, however long or short, are the result of such transactions.

Crises in identity, however, are not inherently evil and should not be feared. Identity conflict arises because one's norms are challenged, especially when individuals from two or more cultures interact. Ting-Toomey and Oetzel (2001) note that every culture has written their own "conflict script" concerning the best way to handle differing expectations for a situation, and frustrations arise when actors have not read the script (p. 11). Cultural research and analysis assists the actors in knowing the best ways to communicate to one another. The goal, the authors relate, is both successfully exchanging information and displaying the proper level of affirmation and respect. In such a way, both communicators recognize and value the other's "face," a term theorists use to describe one's "sense of desired self-worth" (pp. 19-20).

Ting-Toomey (2005) rightly foresees two extremes for the intercultural communicator faced with an identity crisis. First, the communicator may hold too tightly to his or her host culture as the standard by which one judges other cultural values. Such feelings lead to either implied or explicit ethnocentrism. The opposite end of the spectrum involves a complete embrace of the host culture, jettisoning one's given identity entirely. This concept is also undesirable, though, because no one can fully abandon their cultural biases and instead will come to experience what Ting-Toomey (2005) calls "identity chaos" (p. 222). Since neither of these spectrums is optimal, the intercultural communicator must strike a balance between the two through identity negotiation.

Finding a balance in communication style is also the focus within accommodation theory. This sociolinguistic theory states that the conversing parties will "converge to each other's speech characteristics if and when they want to improve communication effectiveness and/or to boost social attractiveness" (Coupland, 2008, p. 268). It is, then, in the best interest for one or both communicators to achieve a successful speech act. Accommodation theory pushes further than identity negotiation theory, however, in claiming that the tension of identity will result at least somewhat in the suppression of one style of communication over the other. Speech and communication becomes, in the view of accommodation theorists like Coupland (2008), a game of dialectic strategy and social consequence (p. 269). Conversant actors seek to empower themselves via their word choice and communicative style, offsetting themselves from others as inferior. For example, a Ph.D. student from the southern United States who is speaking to a colleague from the northern United States may choose to drop their regional accent and use more complex words in order to distance his or herself from the "country bumpkin with no education" stereotype. By doing so, the Ph.D. student is attempting to empower himself in the other speaker's eyes. However, the Ph.D. student cannot stop with merely asserting himself as superior if there is to be successful communication. Some aspects of identity must be laid aside in order for both speakers' identities to be negotiated; thus, the conversation must "converge."

The preceding overview of the theories of identity negotiation and accommodation, however brief, reminds that intercultural communication goals must not be separated from intercultural relationships. Indeed, relationship building and maintaining trusted networks are often just as important in intercultural communicative acts as meeting information goals

(Salacuse, 2010). This is equally true in Romanian culture, where status, personal achievement, and properly approaching a conversation are relationally expected values. As such, it is to this aspect of Romanian cultural values that this study now turns.

Romanian Value Orientations

As mentioned above, Romania became a democracy in 1989. Prior to this date, Romania was under Communist control (1947-1989). The bitter history of Communism is a reality that Romanians are still working through, especially for those who matured during the Communist period. Newly opened historical archives reveal new information each year, reminding Romanians of a past they wish to never relive again. One Romanian historian laments about the Communist period, "The most tragic consequence of that half-century was that it destroyed our *soul*" (Djuvara, 2014, p. 342, emphasis his). Although it has now been almost 30 since Romania's bloody revolution which concluded that time, the road to true democratic transition involves a fundamental worldview shift that is long from over.

Romania's recent entry into the European Union promises an era of increased globalization concerning the nation's values. However, there are multiple value orientations specific to Romania that are worth attention here. The Hofstede Center has published the following graphic, here labeled Figure 1, comparing American and Romanian value orientations.

Figure 1. Value Orientations of the United States compared to Romania.

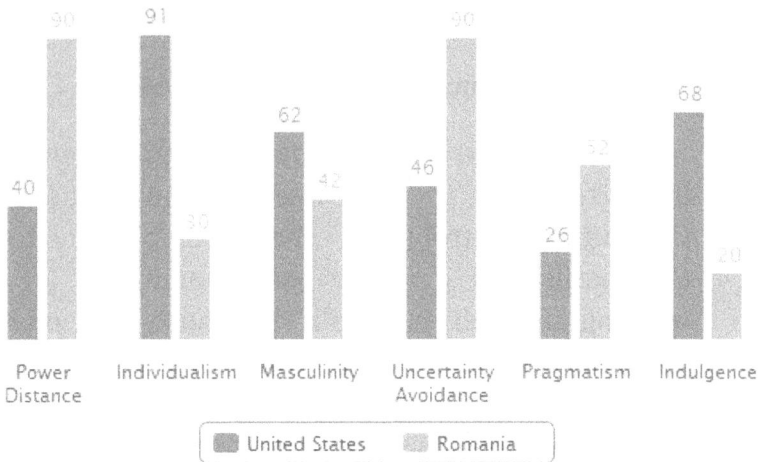

Source: The Hofstede Center. United States in comparison with Romania. Retrieved from http://geert-hofstede.com/united-states.html (accessed December 4, 2017).

The three value orientations with the greatest disparity should be briefly noted. These three orientations are power distance, individualism, and uncertainty avoidance, and each will be examined in turn. Further, using the concepts derived from these orientations will assist in the analysis of my conversation with Adrian.

Power distance refers to the degree to which individuals and organizations accept differences in status, particularly from the view point of lower status members (Hofstede et. al., 2010). High power distance cultures accept inequality as unavoidable fact, whereas low power distance cultures prefer egalitarianism (p. 61). In Hofstede's figure above, Romania scores high on the power distance grid. This means that Romanians are generally comfortable with the fact of inequality among societal members. Special recognition is shown to individuals who have attained higher education degrees, multiple titles and credentials, or elders. The Romanian language reinforces this mentality, with verb forms used to denote status or age. Regular speech, then, perpetuates the role of power distance in the Romanian culture.

In countries exhibiting low power distance, such as the United States, the idea of societal hierarchy is archaic and unacceptable. The traditional breakdowns between parent and child, teacher and student, and elected official and citizen should be equalized as much as possible (Hofstede et. al., 2010, p. 72). In the United States, for example, children will sometimes call adults by their first names, connoting a degree of relational equality that seems strange and disrespectful to members of higher power distance cultures.

Clearly there will be tension when someone from a low power distance culture is immersed in a high power distance culture. I am reminded of the role of power distance in Romania concerning my substitute teaching experience at the Bucharest Baptist Institute last year. Although my Romanian language skills were not great at the time, and I was younger than several students in the class, I was surprised that the students continued to address me using Romanian formal verbs. My initial reaction was to equalize the power distance by personally using the informal tenses, but I soon realized that this would not alter their communication style. Of course, this was merely a sign of respect to the Romanians. My role as teacher, even if only for a two-hour period, solidified the power distance in the room.

The second value orientation to be understood is a culture's degree of individualism. In individualist cultures, personal interests are considered to be of higher importance than group interests. On the other hand, collectivist cultures view group interests higher than personal ones (Hofstede et. al., 2010, p. 90-91). Romania ranks quite low on the individualism scale, displaying that there is a tendency in Romanian culture to think and act as a group. Social ties are strong in collectivist societies, but weak in individual societies (p. 92). On the opposite end of the individualism spectrum resides the United States. Ranking high in individual interests, Americans tend to emphasize personal efficacy, autonomy, and decision-making.

There is indeed a high commitment among Romanians to their personal in-group of family and friends. For example, I once had a conversation with a Romanian girl who expressed a desire to live in another region of the country. When asked why she did not move forward with her plan and begin searching for schools and jobs in the area, she curtly replied, "I cannot go; I have no one there." As an American whose extended family has always lived hours away, this statement shocked me. Unlike my Romanian friend, I had always been taught that following your dreams wherever they took you is the path to success.

Third, the degree of uncertainty avoidance plays a large role in comparing Romanian and American cultures. Uncertainty avoidance refers to a culture's ability to tolerate risk and ambiguity and the need for structure (Hofstede et. al., 2010, 208). Stronger avoidance of uncertainty and ambiguity will result in the formation of more laws, paperwork, and regulations. Romania, as noted above, ranks high in uncertainty avoidance. For example, the process of obtaining a residency permit involves multiple signed documents sent to and from several governmental and non-governmental institutions. Unfortunately, the process of obtaining and substantiating such documents can take months, creating frequent headaches for expatriates.

Although Romania scores considerably high in uncertainty avoidance, the United States locates in the middle percentage-wise. This means that Americans are far less averse to taking risks without clear boundaries in place than their Romanian counterparts, yet there is nevertheless an appreciation for existing rules. In other words, the temptation to progress into uncharted territory is greater in the United States culture than that of Romania.

The three value orientations of power distance, individualism, and uncertainty avoidance clearly differentiate the two cultures of Romania and the

United States, but it would be inaccurate to claim that the comparison graphic represents all Romanians and Americans categorically. Differences among Romanians and Americans may be found due to age, education, region, and intercultural experience. For this reason, it is best to speak of these value orientations in terms of traditional tendencies rather than dominant features. In Romania, there is documented indication that younger employees of businesses are increasingly open to Western styles of lower power distance management and individual responsibility (Aioanei, 2006). Times certainly are changing in Romania.

The opening of Romania to Western ideals, primarily through media outlets, is another locus of cultural shift. Hofstede (2010) helpfully submits that members of collectivist societies with access to the internet are more likely to act on their own behalf than those who do not (p. 124). This idea resonates well in Romanian culture, where greater amounts of younger Romanians have access to high speed internet programs that act as windows to the Western world. All of these elements will now be developed in the latter half of this study, as a conversation with a Romanian named Adrian is analyzed.

Conversation Analysis

Adrian serves as the assistant pastor of one of the largest churches in Bucharest. At age 25, he is also a business entrepreneur, owning and operating a small watchmaking shop in the heart of the city. Though not originally from Bucharest, Adrian moved to the capital several years ago to attend the Baptist Institute, and he has since moved forward to pursue a Master's degree in Baptist Theology. Adrian became a Christian believer in high school and immediately began both interpreting and translating for North American evangelical missionaries and short-term mission teams. In total, Adrian has upwards of ten years of experience working with American evangelicals. This significant fact is evident in the Skype conversation, the transcript of which I have included in Appendix A. Adrian is fluent in spoken English and frequently reads English language books and listens to English language podcasts. In what follows, I will draw from both concepts already defined concerning identity negotiation, accommodation theory, face work, and value orientations, using intercultural pragmatics techniques to draw out analyses of how Adrian negotiates a Romanian-American identity.

Communication in Romania is usually somewhere between high and low context, meaning that a deep understanding of Romanian culture is helpful but not necessary to be able to communicate. This particular conversation is fairly low context because I have not been in Romania since July, and he is merely giving an update on goings-on since we left. Thus there is a fairly relaxed and unassuming tone throughout the twenty minute conversation, owing to Adrian's familiarity with both my wife, Jessica (who is videotaping), and myself. Adrian and I have spent many hours together over the last few years, and thus an informal tone predominates. On a deeper level, though, the careful reader can detect Adrian's familiarity with American communication styles. For example, both Adrian and I affirm one another with the highly informal English slang word "yeah" instead of "yes." The Romanian language does not possess a verbal equivalent for "yeah," only "yes" (Romanian: *da*). "Yeah" is used 17 times by Adrian and by all three of us (including Jessica) a total of 49 times. There is an air of joking and laughter that is uncharacteristic of a high power distance culture, though more common among equals.

In Romanian, the word "yes" is sometimes used as a discourse connector that both links thoughts together and may easily signal the start of a new topic. While this could be the case here, it is more likely that Adrian has picked up the American slang word from his multiple interactions with Americans. He is able to fluidly and securely use this word when speaking in English.

Other slang words that Adrian uses, though less often, are the words "cool" and "awesome." Also using slang words of affirmation, Adrian speaks these particular words when noting either something that has happened, may happen of which he highly approves, or about which he becomes excited. One example is when asked about his recent engagement, where Adrian concludes his story candidly with "That was awesome." The phrase was also turn taking sign, denoting that his narrative was now over, and he is open for new discussion.

Further informality is acknowledged and depicted through our use of vocatives, wherein speakers attract the other communicator's attention. Three times the informal vocative "Hey" is used, once by Jessica to attract Adrian's attention and twice by Adrian to tell a story of how he spoke with other Romanians. While this particular vocative is common in the low power distance culture of the United States, it is much more common for Romanians to use more direct words of address, such as names and participant references, to gather attention. Evident again is Adrian's learned use of American informal address, wherein he is successfully negotiating his identity when speaking with American friends.

Nestled within the conversation are instances of interruption. Some of these cases are due to a poor internet connection; nevertheless, they are significant. For my own part, interruption seems to have occurred when I noticed a lull or pause in conversation flow. At other times, I interrupted Adrian when it seemed like he did not have enough information to give a longer response or if he was looking away from the camera. Adrian, on the other hand, only interrupted once, and that was primarily for subject clarification. This interesting observation seems perhaps to play back into the Romanian value orientation system of uncertainty avoidance. Also a face-saving technique, Adrian did not wish to risk being in the unfortunate position of possibly being told to reenter the conversation and then have to apologize for not taking his turn to begin a new topic. As mentioned above, Romanians prefer to know an activity's boundaries, and in this case Adrian was quite aware that I was the one setting the rules of conversation.

Two other communication techniques may be briefly noted. First, Adrian demonstrates his collectivist tendency through the use of a rhetorical question that is quite common in the Romanian language. When asked to perform a task that he could not, in this case facepainting, Adrian recalls that he said to his pastor friend, "Hey Felix, they're all in United States so what can we do?" This rhetorical question (Romanian: *Ce să facem?*) replaces the blame from one person's fault to the group's, a common feature in Latin-based languages. Second, Adrian is also fond of using doublets, words that carry the same meaning, to add emphasis. Doublets may be found in three distinct places throughout the conversation. Speaking of the reaction to Adrian's engagement story, he says the Americans "cry and show emotion." Later when talking about his desire for David Platt to visit Romania, Adrian admires Platt's "passion and charisma" and that Platt is "really really good" for the International Mission Board. Again, Adrian's doublets do not add meaning to these statements, only emphasis.

Borrowing from identity negotiation theory and accommodation theory, one may conclude that Adrian realizes and accepts that his interests will be better served if he is willing to transition his identity closer to that of an American. Beyond Adrian's obvious knowledge of the global evangelical world, knowledge that he has made clear he possesses, Adrian has adopted several communication tactics to favorably position himself in both Romanian and American communication frameworks. He is neither fully Romanian nor fully American; Adrian is part of the third category of Romanian-American. This is, in fact, the goal of identity negotiation. Ting-Toomey (2005) proposes that true identity negotiators are able to function fluidly in "an 'effortlessly mindful' state," thereby becoming "dynamic cultural transformers" (p. 225). This does not mean that Adrian has fully arrived at this end goal, and I do not believe he would say the same about himself either. He does, however, understand that intercultural communication strategies can be utilized to enhance communication, which is a wise observation in the midst of a fluctuating Romanian culture. Adrian has not embraced American culture to the point of identity chaos, though he has negotiated an identity that is indeed distinct from the traditional Romanian value orientations listed above.

The temptation for Romanians to relinquish their Romanian identity for the promise of economic progress is indeed real. In an article entitled "A 'transatlantic' romance in Romania," Dutu (2004) posits that Romanians have become obsessed with American consumerism and 'McDonaldization,' contributing to a blurred Romanian reality that lies somewhere between perceived and real. Daily life in such a tension can be disturbing, and many Romanians dream of emigration. Another sociologist believes that Romania and other Eastern European nations entering the European Union face this tension on a moral level, primarily because the EU is capable of creating laws to level the moral playing field and redefine "European" morality (Arfire, 2011). Concerning national values, then, Romania is not likely to exit its transitional state anytime soon. In short, what a Romanian like Adrian is left with is the unavoidable reality of identity negotiation. The internet and mass media will continue to bring confrontation for the Romanian people, as multiple value orientations inundate Romanians with every key stroke. The questions for Adrian to consider are how might a Romanian in 2018 find a balance, in Ting-Toomey's (2005) terms, between identity rootedness and identity chaos? How much is too much? Does full accommodation to American cultural norms and communication styles truly bring "the good life"?

Theologian Miroslav Volf (1995) uses the metaphor of "embrace" for the necessity of intercultural communication, because it is in the act of embracing those different than ourselves that we signal to others that we do not wish to be alone any longer (p. 203). Volf is correct. It is only human to communicate, and it is also only human to long to be respectfully understood. Intercultural communication is possible when both parties realize their biases and work toward the accomplishment of both goals and face saving respect. Intercultural communication is successful when both parties can do this without giving away too much of themselves. Through the use of intercultural communication techniques, my Romanian friend Adrian has proven his capacity for dynamic transformation and fluidity. Pragmatic communication analysis, based on this intercultural discussion, demonstrates that Adrian understands the role of facework and value orientations. In addition, Adrian's willingness to navigate the tension of identity negotiation and accommodation indicates mindfulness and respect. Though Adrian will not and cannot fully dismiss his identity, his words and the way he uses them support his intercultural embrace.

Appendix A: Conversation Transcript

11:00 am. Wednesday, November 19, 2014

Skype conversation between Cameron and Adrian, with Jessica videotaping (and sometimes talking):

C: So how are you doing Adrian?

A: So we've been pretty busy. Uh. I mean we have had some events at church – I think you saw some Facebook posts.

C: Yeah. You had the Ireland team, right?

A: Yeah we had the Ireland team. We had the big concert. And we had lots of other events the last couple of months.

C: Yeah.

A: So it's going well.

C: Is everything going well- (Cameron interrupts, though largely due to not hearing well)

A: Jessica's is videoing?

C: Yeah Jessica is videoing. So for this project here, it's called, well the class is called Intercultural Communication. And, uh..

A: What is it called?

C: Intercultural Communication.

A: ... I couldn't hear you.

C: It's called Intercultural Communication.

A: Ok.

C: Does that make sense?

A: Yeah.

C: So I have to like ask someone from my host culture, which is Romania, about...just anything. And then analyze the way that we talk to each other, the communication styles that you use as a Romanian, and that kind of thing.

A: Well, ok. That works.

C: Does that make sense?

A: Yeah, it does. (Adrian looks away and begins moving something that is above his head.)

J: It sort of looks like you're wearing a hat.

A: How does it work? From time to time... Um, I'm going to take a picture of you guys. ‹Pulls out camera› You'll be on my "picture of the day."

C: Cool!

J: Nice!

A: Ok now.

J: Hey, Adrian.

A: Yeah?

J: Can you maybe like move your computer or whatever like a little bit closer to your face so that like your face is bigger?

A: Um. I'll try.... No, I cannot.

C: Yeah. It's ok. So what were you saying before?

A: From time to time it sounds like your voice sounds really robotic (gestures with hand) because the connection. So that is why I'll ask you to repeat something-

C: Yeah. (nodding)

A: Cause if not I don't know if I'll understand your question. Just to know.

C: So how is...

A: Do you have to film the whole project?

J: Yeah.

C: Yeah. But it's ok. It's uh...

A: Poor guy.

C: It's just about a 20 minute conversation. I have to type that up and look at how do you talk about things and that kinda thing. But um...

A: So what is the subject? (interrupting)

C: Well, I mean, I had a couple of things. But first of all, I just wanted to say congratulations on getting engaged!

J: Yeah!

C: You know?

A: Thank you! (gestures with his right hand)

C: We saw your whole video that you posted. It was so cool! (gesturing with both hands)

A: Did you cry? (smiling)

C: Yeah. It was pretty awesome. Pretty awesome.

A: We, we did it that night and we played it for the whole team, you know, from Dallas –

C: Uh-huh.

A: At Sinaia and they all cry and show emotion. I don't know but do Americans tend to cry or something like that or what?

C: It is like sort of. Like usually especially if there is a lot of... Was there a lot of the team a lot of women?

A: If it's what?

C: Were there a lot of women on the team?

A: Yeah they had women but even the guys had like one tear or something.

C: That's hilarious. Yeah. So cool. How did you come up with that idea for that?

A: I'm not sure. (Looking off into distance) I think I was thinking that, um, marriage is like that. Kind of like a bungee jump. You don't actually know what's gonna happen but you have faith that the strap that will hold you back. I guess. I didn't want to do it like wanted to have deep meaning but...yeah. But it went well. She jumped. If she wanted to marry me but didn't have the courage to jump I would have like not posted the video.

C: Yeah. Well that's really cool.

J: You also didn't give her a lot of choice.

A: I...yeah. Hahaha. (Hands covering face) That was awesome.

J: It was really cool.

C: Really cool. So is she...it looks like from your pictures that she's been in Bucharest a lot now. Is that right?

A: Yeah she's been in Bucharest and I've been too..uh...

C: Cluj?

A: Cluj and Baia Mare a lot of times. So we see each other pretty, uh, often. Except for the two or three months when she was in the United States.

C: Ok.

A: Oh. She got her visa for ten years.

J: Nice!

C: Really? Wow!

A: And I got mine and we're coming to States in April for my cousin's wedding.

C: Yeah?

J: Cool.

A: Just in case you were in town or somewhere around. Wait a second, you'll be here. (laughing)

C: We'll be in Bucharest. Yeah...

A: Sorry. We are keeping up with you guys.

C: Yeah it's kinda weird cause we're coming back in just a couple months now. It's kinda surreal, you know?

A: Yeah that will be a really big difference. We're like, "Where's Cameron and Jessica?" We know that you would have really enjoyed some of the projects we did.

J: Yeah.

A: We did face painting in the park combined with other churches. (turns to look directly at camera) And that was a success.

C: Yeah. Where was that at?

A: At one point, the three girls that you worked with for first of June project were all in the United States. Like Maria was in United States, you were in the United States, Carmen was in the United States. And uh, Lindsay...

J: Leslie.

C: Leslie. Yeah.

A: She was in the United States, too.

J: Yeah.

A: I told my friend, "Hey Felix, they're all in United States so what can we do?" So... But Maria came home early. Cause she had to come in like the middle of October...

C: Hmm.

A: But she came at the beginning of September. So...

J: Oh.

A: She was the...yeah she brought her crafts and she taught other four other guys and two or three girls so.

J: Cool.

C: Yeah that's cool. And that was for the 555 thing?

A: Yeah that was for the 555 thing.

C: That's awesome. So did all the churches work together for that?

A: Yeah they did. But we kind of split up in different places of Bucharest and...

C: Yeah.

A: And like we then responded with some feedback. And we had a puppet show. I don't know if you saw the video, did you?

C/J: I don't think so.

A: I'm gonna send it to you on internet. It's on the internet.

J: Ok.

A: It's like short videos. So we have like puppet show and the face painting.

J: Mhmm.

A: And we other churches that, um, went in other parks and then kind of cleaned out the parks and then said something for the kids. And other people prayerwalked.

J: Mhmm.

C: Cool.

A: A lot of people.

C: Was that kind of an effort of all the pastors or all the churches from the group that we met with, or was it bigger than that? (gesturing with both hands)

A: Do you remember I took you to some project to the Bucharest 20/20?

C: Yeah.

A: You know. You know that thing. Now part of the people went to, um, went to, I mean the meeting thing that was- Was it Saturday morning that we went?

C: Yeah.

A: Then they responded as a church.

C: Awesome. Awesome.

A: Now what we didn't succeed to do is the "God's Not Dead" film. Cause they didn't have a license. They said that only in January. Because they said that only it would be ready in January.

C: Ok.

A: And one of my projects was to rent a movie theatre and show it...Just tell me when I should stop talking.

C: No problem. I don't have a set subject, man, I just want to talk to you. It's just nice to talk to you, man.

A: Ok. Cause you know, I can talk a lot.

C: Yeah that's fine. Haha. Yeah that's what they say, you know, that you don't have to really push a preacher to talk all day, you know? (gesturing with both hands)

A: <Laughs> How long...So I've been watching and reading your update things and facebook. You're traveling a lot and in a lot of churches. I even saw a video of you guys on there.

J: Oh I bet it was Eric's.

C: Oh probably yeah. Yeah that was in Ohio.

A: So we follow you guys. Don't worry about us. We're like, "Hey what are they doing?"

J: What state are they in now?

C: What state are they in? How many miles? You know, we have pretty much put about 10,000 miles on our minivan that we're driving. So we've done a lot of traveling.

A: Yeah.

C: Yeah. Cause we have family in Michigan, (hand gesturing) which is in the north, and Florida, which is in the south. And her family's in West Virginia and mine is in Tennessee and we're staying in North Carolina some of the time. So we're driving all over the place, you know. But it's good. We've spoken in, I think, 12 churches now and talked about Romania and had a lot of...you know, I'm talking these two PhD classes now. And we're in California right now, actually. (Short pause indicating change of topics)

J: Oh. Oh you need to tell Adrian the first thing that David Platt said.

C: Oh yeah. So you know David Platt is the new IMB President?

A: Oh I know. I know. Man I'm so jealous when I saw you got to meet him.

C: Well that was last week and so I had never met him like personally before, you know, and so they, they told us like, "You know you should dress up for dinner with the new president. We're not really sure if you have to wear a tie because we're not sure what he's gonna wear or whatever." Can you hear me ok?

A: Yeah I can hear you. Yeah.

C: Ok. So they were like, "Why don't you just wear like a suit coat, like a blazer, like a jacket and a nice shirt but don't worry about a tie cause we're not sure." So then Jessica and I are walking to dinner, you know, and I have my jacket on. And this guy's like, "David Platt is staying in that room there." (gesturing with right hand) And just as we walk by, the door opens to that room and it's David Platt who walks out. So we like introduce (gesturing with both hands) ourselves to him and he's like, "Oh, Cameron, was I supposed to wear a jacket?" <Laughs> And we were like, "Uh, I don't know cause we were supposed to see what you're wearing and then dress accordingly." And so he was like, "I just usually wear jeans, you know?" <Laughs> So it was pretty funny.

A: That is funny.

C: So that was our first encounter with David Platt.

J: Yeah, so he was the only person, the only guy, at the whole dinner that wasn't wearing a jacket.

C: It was hilarious. Really funny.

A: You should definitely bring him to Romania.

C: He said he's never been to Romania before.

J: Yeah we tried to tell him to come. He said he's booked until like April.

A: April?

J: Yeah and then he really wants to spend more time with his family. Like it's kinda crazy for him right now.

C: Yeah he said his family is still living in Birmingham right now. Going back and forth to Richmond, where the IMB Headquarters is, so. (gesturing with both hands) You know and he's got so many pastors and good community members there in Birmingham that it's hard for him to take his family now.

A: How come they chose him for IMB? (looking deeper into camera)

C: Well, they..

A: Cause that's very different for them.

C: Well, you know, they asked us all, you know, what should we be looking for in a new president for IMB? (Start gesturing) Cause the old president, he announced back in like January or something that he was gonna be resigning. And they asked a bunch of people and they asked all of us IMB people what would we be looking for in a new president. And evidently said what I said which was, you know, we need somebody who's able to really catalyze the younger generation. Because a lot of the younger churches in the Southern Baptist Convention are kind of turning away from the IMB because it's seen as too big of a machine, you know, very impersonal. That kind of thing. And so they really took that advice, it sounds like. And David Platt, of course, has such a strong in all of the evangelical world.

A: Yeah I know. Have you heard of Verge?

C: Yeah, Verge Network. Yeah. Did you post the video? I don't know if you posted the video – but somebody posted a video where David Platt and Francis Chan were talking about how, you know, don't let mission become your god. Let God be your God.

A: Oh. I saw it a few days ago but I didn't post it. But I saw it a few days ago.

C: Yeah somebody else posted it. I haven't watched it yet, but...

A: Yeah I mean I really love that guy. They even have his book in Romanian, that...

C: Radical.

A: Radical, yeah. We have that translated.

C: Cool.

A: I'm not sure he's really popular like John Piper would be. Or Francis Chan or others. But we're talking about Romania-

C: Yeah.

A: He's probably more popular in the United States. But we'd really love to have him here.

C: That's cool. Why do you think that –

A: So if you could bring him to Romania that would be awesome.

C: Why do you think he's not as popular in Romania, Adrian?

A: I'm not sure. Uh...(short pause for thought) He wasn't really on media that much like John Piper and all the stuff from different conferences.

C: Do you think that people...(interrupted; could be a connection issue)

A: But his theology and passion and charisma are really cool. And I really like the guy.

C: Yeah.

A: The way he yielded his life. I mean, I think it is a really really good thing for IMB.

C: Yeah, that's for sure.

A: I'm really glad you got the chance to meet him.

C: It's really really cool. He's such a good guy and all. Richard Clark, you know, in Bucharest there, you know, has a nephew at Southern Baptist Seminary in Louisville, Kentucky. (Start gesturing) He said that his nephew is working at the seminary and he said that every time David Platt comes to speak in chapel, Richard's nephew is the one that goes to pick up the chapel speakers from the airport, you know?, and take them to the hotel where Southern Seminary has paid for them for a room and that kinda thing. And, um, evidently when he went to pick up David Platt and took him to the hotel, they parked in front of the hotel and David Platt was like, "What are we doing here? This is too nice of a hotel. You can leave me here but I'm just gonna go somewhere else because this is like a 5 star hotel. I don't want to stay here."

A: (Approving laugh) Hmm. Really?

C: Yeah.

<Conversation continues after recording is stopped>

Elapsed time: 21:00.

CHAPTER FOUR:

EDUCATION IN EASTERN ORTHODOXY

Chills rise up my spine as my friends and I pass through the large doors into the crowded Eastern Orthodox church building. Slowly shuffling along the center of the large single-room chapel, the crowd reluctantly gives way as our Romanian language instructor, Diana, silently indicates that we are to stand near the front in order to better see what is happening. The call-and-response liturgy read melodically by the priests echoes off the white marble floor. Out of the corner of my eye, I see Diana gesture that it is time to kneel while the priest chants verses from the Passion narrative. Upon dropping to my knees, I realize both physically and mentally that this is indeed a new experience for me. I have never before attended an Orthodox service inside a church, teaching me both subtly and overtly in ways quite different than my own tradition.

In this qualitative write-up, I will briefly explain my observations of attending two Eastern Orthodox services during the week preceding Easter. Both services were given entirely in Romanian, and prior to each service I had the honor of interviewing the friend who invited me to attend. Also, one of the priests who conducted the first service was kind enough to allow

85

me to interview him afterward. The testimony from these interviews will be interwoven to add a personal touch to these observations. The observation and interview data will assist in developing a fuller picture of how education works in an Eastern Orthodox church context. While not necessarily engaging with the theology of Orthodox believers, I will note several differences between how education is practiced in Orthodox churches versus in Evangelical ones. This paper will then conclude by offering three primary applications for my own ministry as an evangelical missionary.

Romanians and Eastern Orthodox Christianity

To begin, a short definition of Eastern Orthodoxy is in order. Eastern Orthodox leaders believe that there is an unbroken link between the Early Church and the modern Eastern Orthodox Church. Liturgy, celebration of saints, and tradition, therefore, are precious to the Orthodox believer and must be held closely. Emphasis is placed on the sovereignty and mystery of God, especially when God the Son took on flesh and dwelt among men. It has been said that, whereas Protestant and Catholic Christianity are largely concerned with the personal and knowable aspects of God, Orthodoxy looms large in its concern with the majesty and supremacy of God over humanity. This theme will be returned to often in the course of this analysis, specifically in describing the physical aspects of the Eastern Orthodox church building.

Before delving deeper into the Romanian response to the question of what exactly Christianity means, I will first introduce the three Romanians interviewed. Prior to the first service I attended, I interviewed our language teacher, Diana. Diana is in her mid-30s and grew up in a smaller city in an area known for its stricter adherence to Orthodoxy. Immediately following this first service, I interviewed an Orthodox priest named Vlad. Having served as a "deacon" for three and a half years, Vlad will soon attain the level of full priest after passing some further exams at the five year mark. Vlad also grew up in the same general region as Diana. I will hereafter refer to him as Father Vlad. The third interviewee is our neighbor, Sorin, who is 59 years old and has lived in Bucharest his entire life. Each interview was conducted in Romanian to ensure the interviewee could sufficiently explain their views.

Church Building

As mentioned above, high honor is shown in Orthodox churches to the majesty of God. Upon entering the church, I was immediately struck by the rapt attention the audience maintained before the melodic liturgy being read at the front of the chapel. Several people were kneeling throughout the entire service. One older woman in front of me knelt low for as long as we remained in the building, touching her forehead to the floor in reverent submission before God. At the altar, two priests took turns singing the Scripture and liturgy. The lofty architecture with its high, rounded ceilings seems to reach to the very heavens themselves, and inside the tallest cupola is a mural painting of the Virgin Mary and Jesus Christ. This particular church, known as *Sfântul Danil Sinastrul* (Saint Daniel the Hermit), is not elaborately decorated like some other churches I've seen. Yet still a holy somber silence resounds in the church's vicinity, and I am immediately quieted.

When asked how she feels upon entering an Orthodox church, Diana states, "In the first place, I feel humbled before God, because even though the church is big and very tall, I feel small before God." The architecture is well-suited for the atmosphere of such quiet humility. For Diana, though, there is also a real sense of sadness. When asked to explain why, Diana insightfully responds, "In the sense that these unworthy things are in front of Jesus . . . Even though I know that he died for our salvation, I still perceive in the Orthodox church a feeling that is much more serious and sad. It brings you to a profound meditation, but not joyful, of things." On the one hand, the service is remembering the Last Supper that Christ took with his disciples before Crucifixion, so the mood is not meant to be joyful. Yet Diana is not referring only to this service, but to her overall opinion of entering an Orthodox church.

Sorin goes even further in his explanation of how he feels inside an Orthodox church. For Sorin, while the building itself does inspire "peace and quiet," twice he tells me that he does not feel it is a "magical place, a place where there is accumulated the power of God." The peace and quiet are the most attractive aspects of the church building for Sorin.

Family-based Learning

Most Orthodox believers that I have met are quick to tell me that they learned their faith in the context of family, especially grandparents. All three interviewees, including Father Vlad, affirmed this attitude. Although it was clear Sorin did not want to elaborate after telling me his parents taught him how to observe Orthodox rituals, Diana was happy to give details about how her grandmother would regularly take her to the village church. Although Diana's parents went less frequently, due to their workload, Diana recounts that her grandmother explained how to keep the traditions and norms. Father Vlad remembers well the impact that his grandmother's faith had upon him as a small boy. In her final years, Father Vlad's grandmother was immobilized but maintained a positive attitude and "always always always she would pray."

Kneeling inside the Orthodox church, I look around and see that it indeed consists mostly men and women of my grandparents' age. Inside the crowded church, perhaps 20 people are under the age of 50. Even the midnight Easter service that happened two days later is largely attended by an older constituency. Of course, there are most likely several factors at play in considering why Orthodox services are not well-attended by the younger generations, but there is no need to address that subject here.

Traditions

Another significant component of how Romanians learn to live out their faith is through the practice of Orthodox tradition. While not necessarily taught directly by the priest himself, Romanians know that the Orthodox calendar includes specific "saints days" that are to be celebrated accordingly. At the Thursday evening service I attended, for example, the people around me all seemed fully aware that they were to kneel at each of the twelve readings from the Gospels. Other important traditions within the service consist of crossing oneself, which I noticed being done especially when the priest referenced the Holy Trinity, and gently kissing the Orthodox icons, such as the large, wooden cross brought out by the priests near the conclusion of the service.

When asked how priests use traditions like these to teach people the Orthodox faith, Father Vlad gave the example of praying the prayers of famous saints. Father Vlad's response is so illuminating that he merits being quoted at length.

We have books of prayer in which we have prayers prayed by saints, people who lived many years before our time, but which take us to the place where we need to be found. We can try to pray with our own words, or we could try to say things as we see them, very good, but these things are not actually as they seem to us. We cannot recognize from the start how we really are, what is our state, how we stand, what I've done well, what I've done wrong. There are many people who come to church for confession to confess their sins and say, "I haven't done anything wrong." They do not realize it. It is hard to realize it when you do wrong. So therefore we have all kinds of prayers and spiritual rhythms which teach us from where we are starting, where we stand.

Praying saints' prayers, then, helps Orthodox believers better see reality, knowing more precisely how to understand themselves before God. This is but one tool priests may offer the general population in growing more mature in their faith.

For the sake of space, I will now transition to the second and final section of this analysis. I begin by offering three differences between educational practices in Eastern Orthodoxy and that of Protestantism. Second, I will relate three possible areas in which Eastern Orthodox education practice may be applied in Protestant churches.

Orthodox and Evangelical Education in Dialogue

Three differences between educational practices in Eastern Orthodoxy and Evangelicalism include the overall attitude and posture of participants, use of ritual and tradition, and oral versus literate learning techniques. First, the difference in overall attitude and posture of Orthodox and evangelical churches is often well-pronounced, especially in Romania. As mentioned above, Orthodox churches are tall edifices with beautiful architecture and icons. Likewise, Orthodox believers adopt a quiet, humble posture before the Almighty God, standing and kneeling as the service progresses. Orthodox priests read the liturgy in singsong voices that may or may not be projected by sound equipment. Evangelical churches are usually equipped with chairs or benches for participants, encourage believers to sing and pray together, and a church leader speaks a message that is meant to be practical and understandable. The tone is generally considered more lively and welcoming in an evangelical church, while at the same time lacking the longstanding history of the Orthodox service.

Second, the Orthodox use of ritual and tradition to teach consistency is largely rejected in evangelical circles. Indeed, tradition is placed on par with Scripture for the Orthodox in terms of significance. Saints days are observed, and many of the more widely known saints days are celebrated with specific types of food and prayers. Veneration of icons also plays an important role, since many Romanian Orthodox believers display an icon or two in their homes. Evangelicals also have traditions, such as praying before meals, but they are not held at the same level as the Orthodox Church and are often culturally-based.

Third, differences exist in teaching concerning oral and literate learning styles. The evangelical tradition largely emphasizes literate learning models, believing firmly that people should be able to read God's word for themselves in order to know how to live. Evangelical services climax in the reading and preaching of God's written word, symbolized by the pulpit placed in the front and center of the church. In contrast, much of the Orthodox tradition utilizes oral-based learning methods. While true that the priests read the liturgy during services, the entire experience is targeted at all five senses: smelling the incense, hearing the melodic voice of the priest, touching the ground and icons, seeing the beautifully-painted pictures, and tasting with the brush of the lips the icons set along the margins of the church. Orthodox believers are thus taught that their services are holistic, which is far more oral than literate as a concept.

With these three differences in mind, there are also at least three ways in which those from an evangelical tradition might learn in regards to education. The three ways of learning to educate stem directly from the differences. First, evangelicals would do well to learn from the Orthodox emphasis on humility before God. Too often it seems that evangelical leaders make God out to be so personal that they miss the majesty of God. The reverence I felt in both Orthodox services which I attended was stirring and gave me pause in considering how I think about God. True, God is a friend of sinners who sticks closer than a brother, yet God is also sovereign over all He has created, and no one can stand in God's presence without an intermediary. Personally, it was good for my heart to kneel physically, not simply just bow my head and close my eyes. Evangelical Christians would do well to recall in wonder the magnificence of the Godhead and enact actual times within their services to physically demonstrate their smallness before the throne.

Second, the Orthodox use of ritual and tradition is an important part of being Christian. While the Bible is clear, of course, that there is no salvific gain, remembering the past can only help in safeguarding one's faith in the present. To know that a Christian stands in a long line of others who also lived and practiced their faith the same way is important. In many areas, evangelicals have lost this respect for the past. I was impressed by Father Vlad's answer when I asked him what Christianity means to him. Father Vlad said, "Christianity for me and for my parents and for our people means, above all else, the religions of our parents and grandparents."

Third, the Orthodox inclusion of oral learners is significant and should be incorporated by evangelical leaders for maximum impact. Unfortunately, most evangelical leaders and missionaries use highly literate means to appeal to the oral majority. According to scholars such as Lovejoy (2012), men and women who prefer oral learning methods could be as large as 80% of the world population (p. 29). The holistic emphasis on Christian teaching in the Orthodox Church, geared toward using all five senses in worship, is helpful because it demonstrates that believers with learning styles different from the primary leader also should be integrated in worship. Every gesture, melody, movement, and rhythm dynamically retells the story of how God relates to his people. This is not to say that evangelicals should give up their emphasis on reading and interpreting the Bible, but there should also include more oral elements that may assist in bringing balance to the oral-literate divide.

Conclusion

Education in Romania's version of Eastern Orthodoxy is based largely on tradition and repeated ritual; both priest and lay believer are caught up in the mystery of worshipping the Almighty God. Through the use of oral-based methods that mostly remain unchanged for centuries, families are responsible for passing along the faith. Evangelical Christians like myself have much to learn from Orthodox education practices, especially concerning the holistic approach of faith-based learning.

As the clock strikes midnight and the bells toll above the masses, signaling the beginning of Easter Sunday, I look over at my Orthodox neighbor, Sorin. With his candle held tightly in both hands, Sorin waits expectantly for the church doors to open and the priests to exit and address the crowd. Suddenly the doors fling open and out step the priests in white robes, who only minutes before donned only black. Beginning with the priest, each candle is lit one-by-one and the light flickers brightly in the night. After a brief liturgy, the priest leads us all three times in the familiar Easter chorus:

Hristos a înviat din morţi	Christ is risen from the dead
Cu moartea pe moarte călcând	Trampling death with death
Şi celor din morminte	And to those in the graves
Viaţa dăruindu-le.	Giving them life.

Following this amazing chorus, which everyone knows, the priest then begins the three-fold call-and-response:

Hristos a înviat!	Christ is risen!
Adevărat a înviat!	He is risen indeed!

CHAPTER FIVE:

ORTHODOX BACKGROUND BELIEVERS:

LISTENING AND LEARNING[1]

My stomach must have growled rather loudly. The Romanian Orthodox monk speaking with my wife and me kindly finished his sentence and invited us into the monastery's quaint kitchen to continue our conversation over lunch. Visibly stunned and at a loss for words, my wife politely accepted, and soon we sat speaking over a meal of lentil soup and fish. The monk and I exchanged a cordial back-and-forth conversation about the differences between Orthodox and Protestant Evangelical theology; both of us admittedly surprised by the competence in explaining our own religious traditions and respectful grasp of the other's. Before becoming a monk at the famous Putna Monastery, Father Andrei had studied law in Bucharest and visited multiple Protestant churches. As I recall that unique lunch from two years ago, one phrase spoken by the monk reverberates in my mind: "I

---

[1]This essay was originally published in Armstrong, Cameron D. (2017). Orthodox background believers: Listening and learning. *Great Commission Research Journal* 9(1): 81-92.

appreciated the Protestant emphasis on the Bible, but as I looked around at the Romanians worshipping in those churches, I could not help but think they were turning their back on their culture."

Father Andrei's thoughts are indicative of how, for many Romanians, turning from Orthodoxy to another religious tradition involves a certain degree of cultural transformation. No longer do Romanians behave and worship the same way, and the results are certainly noticeable to friends and family. Following the social science definition of Harrison & Hunter (2000) that "culture" is the sum total of a society's underlying attitudes, values, and beliefs, the mental and practical transformation that takes place after one shifts from Orthodoxy to evangelicalism may be considered cultural in nature (p. xv). Such cultural transformation is what Protestants call *conversion*, since it is foundationally a religious decision that is worked out in one's value system and subsequent life choices.

Unfortunately, little research exists exploring the issue of how Romanian evangelicals with an Orthodox background came to the decision to convert. In my research, I could find only one source on the subject, and even that deals only with Orthodox theology in evangelism (Spann, 2001). Therefore, the following study is intended to begin filling this gap, based on interviews with four Orthodox Background Believers (OBBs). I will first offer a broad-brush picture of the situation of Orthodoxy and evangelicalism in Romania. Then I delineate five major themes drawn from in-depth, semi-structured interviews with four OBBs, whom I will call Mihai, Iosif, Mihaela, and Diana. Finally, I conclude by sketching a potential "evangelism rubric" that evangelical churches may use in their outreach to Orthodox people.

Orthodoxy and Evangelicalism in Romania

According to the 2011 census, Romania is 86% Eastern Orthodox, or simply Orthodox. Further breakdown by the National Institute of Statistics Romania (2013) declares that evangelicals make up roughly 6% of the population. Yet the 6% figure also includes groups such as Jehovah's Witnesses and Unitarians (p. 4). Eastern Orthodoxy in Romania goes back thousands of years to the first few centuries after Jesus' death. Longstanding tradition, emphasis on the mystery of God, and the Orthodox desire to ignite all five senses (touch, taste, sight, hearing, smell) make Orthodox services exceptionally memorable and powerful (Fairbairn, 2002). Evangelicalism in Romania, on the other hand, is only about 500 years old, having taken a foothold a generation or so after the Protestant Reformation began in 1517 in Central Europe (Hitchins, 2014). From its inception, the evangelical movement has upheld biblical authority as central, often advocating a renunciation of art and imagination in response to excesses in Catholicism and Orthodoxy. The evangelical tenet of *sola Scriptura* makes for undeniably passionate preaching.

Theologically speaking, perhaps the most significant distinction between Orthodoxy and evangelicalism is the concept of personal choice. According to Orthodox doctrine, a person becomes an Orthodox Christian through baptism (St. Athanasius Orthodox Academy, 1993, p. 217). Baptism is usually done for infants in Orthodox homes. In contrast, evangelical Christians maintain that people must be old enough to choose for themselves whether or not they wish to believe and be baptized (Letham, 2007). For the purposes of this study, however, I have chosen not to interact with Orthodox theology. Only at certain points while developing common themes from my interviews will I delve a bit into Orthodox belief. Multiple reliable resources are available to explain key theological differences (Fairbairn, 2002; Letham, 2007). In this analysis I am especially concerned with Orthodox versus evangelical behavioral practice, specifically in conjunction with the conversion process.

A recent study by the Pew Foundation classifies the Orthodox countries of Eastern Europe as "believing and belonging, without behaving" (Pew Research Center, 2017). In other words, less value is placed on living according to Eastern Orthodox ethics as to that of mentally believing that one's religious affiliation to Orthodoxy defines them culturally. In essence, this landmark study gives hard data demonstrating the old adage: "To be Romanian is to be Orthodox."

Yet, as the following themes from the interviews explain, the practical application of Orthodox theology is often lacking among its adherents. Such desires for moral living were in large part what initially drew the interviewees to seek God in evangelical expressions. As mentioned above, however, conversion from the majority faith to a minority faith is not without price. Thus family ties among OBBs become strained or even severed, as OBBs are sometimes mocked for renouncing their "Romanian-ness" for a Western-looking minority faith.

Meet the Evangelical Christians

Before developing the major themes that arose out of the interviews, it would be helpful to give a brief word about the interviewees themselves. Further detail will be given below in the five subsequent themes. Doing so assists in limiting the study's findings to Romanian men and women of similar age ranges, namely 20-35 years old. Also, for the sake of anonymity, names have been changed.

Mihai is 30 years old and became an evangelical Christian at the age of 14. Before becoming an evangelical Christian, Mihai's family rarely went to church and hardly ever spoke about Christianity. Following the dramatic lifestyle change brought about by his father's conversion, Mihai slowly began the process for himself. Although an introvert, Mihai now avidly serves in his church's worship music team and enjoys aiding others in exploring how to share the gospel in the workplace.

Iosif works for an evangelical Christian organization. In his early 30s, Iosif converted out of Orthodoxy at 19 in what he describes as "a process" that first began with his older sister's conversion. After his own conversion, Iosif's family quickly noticed his regard for a more moral lifestyle, and although they did not become evangelicals themselves, Iosif's parents did encourage him forward. A hard worker with a strong passion for evangelism and university students, Iosif lives to see Romanians reached with the life-changing message of the gospel.

Working as a psychologist among special needs children, *Mihaela* is 31 years old and became an evangelical believer as a teenager. Strained relationships, specifically with her parents and former boyfriends, caused Mihaela to have an "up and down" journey toward full commitment to God and the evangelical expression of Christianity. Besides working with children, Mihaela's passion is to reach other Romanian women wrestling with abusive relationships.

The final interviewee, *Diana,* is 23 and became an evangelical Christian only two years ago. After the death of her beloved grandfather, with whom Diana lived for many years, solace was found in going to church and reading the Bible. Like Mihaela, however, Diana's parents do not understand why she converted, although they have slowly begun to accept her lifestyle change. To date, Diana has not been baptized as an evangelical believer, but wishes to soon.

Conversion Themes

As mentioned above, five common themes arise from the interviews I have conducted with Mihai, Iosif, Mihaela, and Diana. The themes are (1) influence of a near acquaintance, (2) existing spiritual interest, (3) frightening life crises, (4) desire for community, and (5) acceptance by immediate family. On the whole, these themes also appeared in this order in each interviewee's conversion narrative. Each theme will be discussed in turn.

Theme One: Influence of a near acquaintance.

Interestingly, each interviewee maintains that a family member or close friend was instrumental in first introducing them to evangelical Christianity. Mihai recalls that, after his father changed jobs, some evangelical Christian coworkers attending the local Baptist church first invited him. Afterward, Mihai's father began attending regularly and slowly began renouncing his alcohol addiction. In Romania, consuming alcohol is taboo for evangelical Christians. Obviously, this delighted Mihai's mother, who had borne the brunt of her husband's alcoholic fury for years. So she happily obliged when her husband asked to bring Mihai and his mother to the Baptist church. Mihai humorously admits that at first he was "dragged along" and felt the three hour service intolerable.

For Iosif, the noticeable conversion of his older sister to evangelical Christianity left a strong impression on his teenage self. Although the sister would not forcefully preach at him about going to hell or eternal damnation, Iosif's sister would often ask him questions and ask him to read from the Bible or other biblically-based literature. Slowly Iosif did begin reading the Bible for himself and considering his sister's words. Like Mihai, however, it was the visible change of his family member that found its mark.

Both female interviewees, Mihaela and Diana, trace their initial introduction to the evangelical community through close childhood friends. For Mihaela, the kindness of two evangelical classmates attracted her to their church. Diana's best friend took her to church after the tragic death of Diana's grandfather and also encouraged her to attend an evangelical church in Bucharest, where she attends university. Although their conversion stories are by no means the same, Mihaela and Diana find a kinship in a similar journey to finding God.

Theme Two: Existing spiritual interest.

Every narrative reached back to the time before the interviewees' conversion, and one by one there was evidence of spiritual interest from childhood. Even though each family showed little to no interest in discussing spiritual matters or going to church beyond Christmas and Easter, the four men and women I spoke with thought deeply about the supernatural. Mihai explains that, because Orthodox religion was taught in school, and sometimes the class would attend a nearby

Orthodox church, the reality of hell often echoed in his mind. Generally the class would be asked to confess their sins to the priest, but Mihai would become frightened that God would damn him for an unconfessed sin. "And the older I got, the more scared I would get," Mihai remembers sadly.

Diana also recalls going from time to time as a child to the Orthodox church to confess sins, although her attitude was somewhat more critical than Mihai's towards confession. Diana observes that she was always interested in God, but after the eighth grade she gave up trying to figure out how to live Christianly. All that changed, of course, when her grandfather died. Pausing for a moment, Diana summarizes: "I felt hopeless. I mean all those emotions that I kept for all those years just like blew away. So I always told to my best friend, 'I have a hole.'" Such hopelessness led Diana's friend to invite her to church, where the healing process began.

Iosif and Mihaela have little memory of attending the Orthodox church, especially with their parents. Once, Mihaela lived with her grandmother for a time, and they would always attend the Orthodox church together. All her life, however, Mihaela had a sense that the evangelical church taught the truth and was "always convinced that one day I would repent." Growing up, Iosif only went to the Orthodox church "once or twice a year, during Easter," but beyond learning the Lord's Prayer, religion was not discussed in the home. Yet after Iosif's sister became an evangelical Christian, Iosif entered a multiple-year period of wrestling with the desire to also convert.

Theme Three: Frightening life crises.

Each interviewee became quiet for a moment recalling the awe of a frightening life event that ultimately led to their conversion. Because these events make up such a strong portion of each interviewee's narrative, I will spend considerable more time relating them. Further, such crises may be considered the "crescendo" of the transformations.

After attending the Baptist church for several months, Mihai was asked to attend a nearby evangelical Christian camp. Excited, Mihai smilingly tells of the massive tents for the campers and well-trimmed soccer fields and volleyball courts. Says Mihai, "I found it awkward at first. We had prayer groups in the mornings and the afternoons. We prayed before each dinner. We sang weird songs. I guess by that time I was getting used to it." The week-long camp culminated on a stormy Thursday evening, in which the camp preacher spoke about Christ dying for the sins that are taking people to hell. Mihai again, "I was like, 'I know that. I can't do anything about it.' And then he said that we can have a relationship with God and talk to Him and ask Him to forgive our sins and that's all we need to do. And by believing that he can and will forgive our sins, then that's it." So when the altar call came and the group was asked who would like to take this step, Mihai quickly said yes. Mihai's fears of an inescapable hell instantly dissipated. Mihai vividly adds that immediately the storm ceased and the sun came out, and "it was like redemption in nature. Quite symbolic."

Iosif also attended an evangelical Christian camp in high school but, though he enjoyed the clean fun, he still wanted to "be free and see the world." After years of wrestling with the claims of the Bible and the truth of his sister's words, it all came to a head his first year of college. Although he liked to attend the meetings of a Christian organization for students, Iosif would often leave the meetings and go directly to partying and drinking with his friends. At one point, one of Iosif's friends was beat up and spent time in the hospital. After his friends retaliated, Iosif was caught in the crossfire of a battle between his friends and some older students. One night, some "scary guys" came looking for him to beat him up, thinking that he was part of the retaliating group. Says Iosif, "And that was the moment that I got scared for my life. I looked at my life and saw that I was a mess inside . . . I was like humbled in a way through that situation and I think that was the moment when I said I really want to follow God with all my heart." Iosif gave up drinking and became even more involved with the campus Christian organization, finding happiness in his new life.

Mihaela's "frightening event" occurred after multiple harsh relationships with abusive men. One particular boyfriend appeared to be a faithful Orthodox Christian, even taking interest in Mihaela's fixation with evangelical Christianity. It soon became clear, however, that Mihaela's boyfriend actually had psychological problems. At one point he even threatened to commit suicide. Three times Mihaela asked God to give her a sign that she should break up with him, and after God provided precisely what she requested, she finally did. "It was hard because I felt guilty before God and thought God was punishing me because I wasn't helping him," Mihaela whispers. In the end, after hours spent with both evangelical Christian friends and in personal Bible study, Mihaela proudly exclaims, "I got better all the way." And, as mentioned above, Mihaela now views her role in God's Kingdom as helping other women escape from similar pasts.

Finally, Diana's world was turned upside down with the death of her grandfather. Having grown up with him living in the same house, Diana believes that her grandfather's death truly set her on the trajectory to life in Jesus. When she first entered her friend's church, Diana recalls beautifully, "I felt like a peace inside me. I felt like the pain on my shoulders just went away. Finally I felt happy and alive, because before that I didn't feel alive, kind of like a robot." Diana began reading her Bible regularly with a fervent desire. She also began attending an evangelical church every Sunday, where she appreciates the fervor and continues to grow in her devotion to her newfound faith.

Theme Four: Desire for community.

Another common thread among each conversion story is the strong desire to be part of a faith community. After each interviewee's conversion experience, it became clear to them that they needed to be around other like-minded people. Perhaps the most striking examples of the four interviews come from the narratives of Iosif and Mihaela.

After attending the evangelical Christian camp in high school, seeing normal guys and girls who appeared especially genuine in their faith, Iosif said to himself, "Yeah, maybe I want to try this." Further, Iosif continued attending the prayer meetings of a campus evangelical Christian organization, participating in their events and enjoying the pleasant atmosphere that he did not find elsewhere.

Mihaela, too, notes how she kept coming back to evangelical churches after every rough and humiliating experience. In her youth, Mihaela's parents physically restrained her from joining an evangelical church, even declaring that she would have to move out if she tried. Now, Mihaela is deeply committed to her evangelical church and friends.

Theme Five: Immediate family acceptance.

While baptism in an evangelical church constitutes a stark rip from one's Orthodox background, it is interesting that each interviewee finds that their immediate family members slowly began to accept their new identity. Their parents may not comprehend the decision to convert, much less desire to follow, but yet they have come to appreciate the positive effect the conversion has made. Of course, for Mihai, his parents' conversion played an integral role in his own, since they all joined the evangelical church at roughly the same time. Mihai's Orthodox relatives may not fully understand the change, but they clearly notice differences in Mihai's family's actions. For example, Mihai's father gave up drinking, often prays aloud at family gatherings, and loves to talk about Christianity.

The dramatic change brought about in Iosif's life as a result of his conversion gave his parents great pause. Iosif recalls that, even though they did not attend, his mother became so excited about his giving up alcohol and exorbitant lifestyle that she would often wake him up on Sunday so as not to be late for the evangelical church. Also, Iosif's father, who said he'd never enter an evangelical church, came to see him be baptized. And, of course, Iosif's older sister encouraged him every step of the way, and even today Iosif's family and his sister's family attend the same church and remain close.

Mihaela's parents are not evangelical believers, either, but cannot help but wonder at the remarkable way Mihaela's life has turned around. From living in fear and guilt in abusive relationships to exhibiting the confidence of a Christian woman with impeccable intelligence, Mihaela's mother and father are proud of their daughter. Unfortunately, Mihaela's father still struggles with alcohol, and her mother wants nothing personally to do with Christianity. But Mihaela's father did attend her baptism, even though it was several hours' train ride, out of both fascination and love for his daughter.

Like Mihaela, Diana's parents show little signs of interest in evangelical Christianity. Each time Diana returns to her hometown during a break from university, she knows questions about her faith may pop up. Diana relays, "But they've kind of started to accept that I'm going [to the evangelical church] . . . They tell me I'm different. Like, 'you are not you.' It's like, 'What? But I'm still me.' Yeah, I think the way I think and the way I act is different from what I used to. Now I kind of know what I believe."

To summarize this section on the five themes, several propositions are clear. (1) Near acquaintances, specifically family members, greatly influenced the conversion of OBBs. (2) The OBBs interviewed already maintained a heightened awareness to spiritual matters. (3) Frightening life crises ultimately led to making the conversion decision. (4) Desire was strong for a healthy community that took seriously the call to ethical living. (5) Acceptance by immediate family members, based on the sustained positive change of lifestyle, assists the OBB because they do not have to deal with a clean, full break from family.

Potential Evangelism Rubric

Based on the common themes gleaned from interviews with the four OBBs, I offer the following "evangelism rubric." Ideally, the rubric could potentially be used by evangelical churches and organizations in outreach. The evangelism rubric sets as its foundation two key Bible verses (1 Pet. 3:15 and 2 Cor. 2:15) that uphold both the need for effective spoken evangelism and ethical Christian practice. Each element will be briefly explained below.

Reproducible Evangelism Rubric in Majority-Orthodox Romania

	Poor	Fair	Strong
Relationships with Orthodox neighbors			
Biblically-centered worship services			
Knowledge of gospel			
Ability to articulate gospel/testimony in non-churchy words			
Judgment-free atmosphere			
Enjoyable outreach activities			
Transparent relationships			
Ethical living among members			

Verbal Evangelism (Word)   **Ethical living (Deed)**

Always be prepared to give an answer to everyone who asks you to give a reason for the hope that you have. 1 Peter 3:15

For we are to God the pleasing aroma of Christ among those who are being saved and those who are perishing. 2 Corinthians 2:15

Based on the twin realities that spoken evangelism should be confirmed through ethical Christian living (Litfin, 2012), evangelical churches and organizations seeking to reach Orthodox people with the gospel may use this grid to evaluate their practices. Leaders should ask if their members maintain a solid witness in both areas by working through the rubric's eight elements. Yet before giving a quick description of each element, it should be noted that I do not claim the list to be exhaustive; nor are the elements placed in a specific order of gradation. The rubric is merely offered as a response to the interviews and should be adapted as further research becomes available.

Moving from bottom-to-top, churches should evaluate to what degree their members *live ethically* according to Scripture. Each interviewee noted fondly how they found a high degree of ethical living in the evangelical churches they visited, which was quite attractive. *Transparent relationships* refers to the extent that church members are willing to allow one another into their whole lives. Seeking an authentic, faith-based community both drove the OBBs to search for and continue in the evangelical church. Especially younger generations, like those interviewed, long for communities that are not filled with "professional Christians," but instead made up of men, women, and children ready to learn and grow together.

Both Mihai and Iosif joyfully place evangelical Christian camps as central to their conversion journey.

Evangelical churches and organizations should cultivate other *enjoyable outreach activities,* where both introverts and extroverts, young and old can have clean fun that is also attractive to non-evangelicals. Likewise, evangelical churches should cultivate a *non-judgmental atmosphere* in which all types of people are welcome and feel comfortable. Also related to atmosphere is church members' ability to use *non-churchy words* as they interact with non-evangelicals, adding to the comfort level of all and eliminating potentially-awkward insider vs. outsider conversation. Especially in communicating the gospel and the story of one's conversion to evangelical Christianity, non-evangelicals are often found scratching their heads in confusion due to the "insider language" of the evangelical church. Regrettably, insider, "churchy" talk made both Mihai and Iosif uncomfortable for a time when they first entered the evangelical church.

Next on the rubric is the element of *knowledge of the gospel,* returning to one's ability to know and articulate the transforming message of Jesus Christ. Preaching should be geared towards church members being able to reproduce in their own words what was delivered on Sunday, so that those outside the evangelical community may hear and be saved. For example, each interviewee was initially astounded at the simplicity of believing that Christ's sacrifice atones once and for all for sins, and thus the doctrine of complete forgiveness should be majored on. As Mihai brilliantly put it, "It's like you go to school and there's this huge bully that you know you'll meet at the end of classes, and there's no avoiding it. But at one point along the way here comes a huger guy that can beat up the bully." *Biblically-centered worship services* need be just that, centered on the Scripture and not on putting on a show that will attract as many new people as possible. It is God's Word that pricks hearts, as evidenced by the testimonies of those interviewed.

Finally, if an evangelical church desires to increase their outreach to Orthodox people, leaders must encourage and model the maintenance of *relationships with Orthodox neighbors*. It is because of evangelical Christians like Mihai's father's coworkers and Iosif's sister and Mihaela's schoolmates and Diana's best friend that the process of turning to evangelical Christianity was begun. These believers were willing to become personally involved in the lives of their Orthodox friends and family, allowing their Orthodox neighbors to watch up close how they lived out their faith. Evangelical Christians would do well to remember, as expressed by Van De Poll & Appleton (2015), "people need time to find out what the Christian faith means in their life situation" (p. 5).

I propose this evangelism rubric for evangelical church and organizational leaders to seriously evaluate both themselves and their membership. Again, it is by no means an exhaustive list. Yet using this rubric could be a solid first step in understanding what areas leaders need to focus on if outreach to Orthodox people is truly an objective.

Conclusion

Interviewing these OBB friends was not a chore for me. Indeed, it is an honor to recount their conversion stories. Due to their unique background in the Orthodox tradition, OBBs are poised to assist evangelical Christians in understanding how to conduct outreach, if only leaders might take the time to listen. This paper may be considered a "first step" in that direction.

Returning to my experience at Putna Monastery, the winsome Orthodox monk with whom we had lunch maintained that to give up on Orthodoxy is to change cultures. In the sense that conversion is a change of values, beliefs, and assumptions, the monk is quite right. But that is not how OBBs see it. They are still Romanian, with a common language and heritage like any Romanian Orthodox person. Yet, as Diana says, "But I'm still me. Yeah, I think the way I think and the way I act is different from what I used to. Now I kind of know what I believe." What has changed is conversion; the cross-over evangelicals aptly call a "new birth."

CHAPTER SIX:

HONOR AND SHAME:

CROSS-CURRENTS IN ROMANIAN
CULTURE[1]

The booing started with roughly twenty minutes left on the clock. Never in my life had I ever seen a home team being booed, yelled at, and scorned. The Romanian national football (soccer) team played an incredible first half, routing Finland's finest like they were enjoying it, and causing the national stadium to buzz with excitement. Yet, a few minutes into the second half, the Finns scored and the excitement rapidly morphed into discouragement. Based on experience in the United States, my friends and I expected at any moment that the crowd would erupt in encouraging cheers for their hometown heroes. Instead, thousands of disgruntled Romanians began shouting and shuffling for the exits. Shocked and unnerved, we quietly watched as the Romanian team reacted with somewhat downcast faces. Their

---

[1]This essay was originally published in Armstrong, Cameron D. (2015). Honor and shame cross-currents in Romanian culture. *Jurnal Teologic, 14*(2), 95-123.

countrymen have turned on them, we thought, giving up on them with several minutes left to tie the game. The commotion only grew louder as the play clock wound down. Miraculously, the Romanians scored in the final seconds and won back their neighbors' shattered favor. Speaking with Romanian friends about this odd occurrence, I discovered that such methods of shaming people in order to motivate them are the norm. Indeed, my Romanian colleagues were themselves surprised to find that Americans do not use shame tactics like this at sporting events.

Though not generally viewed in this light, Romanians exhibit multiple indicators of an honor-shame culture. In fact, a far greater emphasis is placed on shame in Romanian culture than honor. Analysis concerning this implicit nature will be of value to anyone working with Romanians at all levels. In what follows, I will first outline the honor and shame worldview structure. Afterward, I will analyze several areas wherein Romanian culture displays these tendencies, interweaving personal stories and testimonies from Romanians themselves. I will then conclude by offering several ways in which these values might be defined in terms of a Romanian worldview.

Honor and Shame as a Value System

To begin, cultural anthropologists often associate certain world regions with particular value systems. Two broad categories are accepted in the discussion concerning culture-specific values: individualist and collectivist (Livermore, 2009, 123). Individualistic cultures consider individual people capable of making their own decisions and owning their own consequences. Choices are made because the end goal seems attractive to the individual decision-maker. Concepts of right and wrong, then, stem from one's own consciousness and moral understanding. In an individualist society, results considered good or evil by the masses are a reflection of individuals making their own decisions and forging their own paths. The most blatantly individualistic cultures are generally considered those found in the Global West.

The anthropological term denoted to individualistic cultural value systems is innocence and guilt (IG). Psychologically speaking, individualists view themselves as inherently separated from the choices they must make. Good choices will result in favorable rewards for the individual. For example, I am writing this paper because I chose to attend this class, fulfill its requirements, and attain a positive grade. I am not at all worried about whether or not my classmates write their own papers because in no way does that reflect my performance. If my colleagues receive poor marks on their papers, it is not my fault. *They are the ones that did not do what they were supposed to do. I am innocent.* This line of thinking is quite individualistic and points toward my cultural background as an American.

On the other hand, most of the world's cultures are collectivistic. In a collectivist culture, group opinion is vital in the making of decisions and the sharing of resources. Richards & O'Brien (2012) helpfully explain that collectivist cultures are concerned chiefly with the preservation of communal harmony and finding one's identity within the larger community (p. 97). Contrasted with the IG paradigm, cultures found in the Middle and Far East tend toward a system of honor and shame (HS). Wu (2012) describes how this reality is based on group members' abilities to conform to a set standard of right and wrong. If men and women conform to the group's standards, they will be reward through being shown extra value in the eyes of others. This idea of attributing value is defined as "honor." Likewise, lack of conformity results in a public devaluing of group members, and is termed "shame" (Wu, 2012, p. 148-151). And shame in the eyes of one's community ripples further than most Westerners can know.

Again, the major difference revolves around who is the one capable of making value judgments: the member themselves or the entire group? If someone hailing from a culture with a IG paradigm is terminated from their employment, others from the same culture might respond, "She continued doing bad things. She'll learn." If that same someone grew up in an HS system, the response would most likely involve, "She did those things because she is a bad person." Obviously, each scenario will produce different results in the face of the terminated girl's community. IG views the chooser and the choice separately; HS says the two are inherently connected. IG is about *doing* the right thing as defined by written codes; HS is about *being* the right thing as defined by society.

Of course, one cannot be anything besides himself or herself. Each individual must act according to how they wish to be rewarded. In HS cultures, therefore, honor acts as a form of currency that is to be publicly distributed to the worthy. Just as money is a limited good, likewise only particular amounts of attainable honor are available. One must work to retain their honor, meaning that their relationship to those around them is at stake every day. Failure to live up to others' standards results in shame, and this outcome causes the one who is shamed to internalize societal views. Flanders (2011) writes, "Thus, the distinguishing mark of a shame culture is a dependence upon what others think" (p. 58). Further, one's public projection of self is termed "face," and it is in the world of "facework" where members are honored and shamed. Every conversation is seen as an opportunity to properly or improperly show honor.

Let us return briefly to the example offered above concerning my class paper. As mentioned above, because I tend toward the IG worldview, I need not concern myself with the thoughts of my classmates. Intrinsically, I approach my computer thinking, "I will write this paper because I want a good grade." Sure, I might be interested to see what grades others receive, but this would be after the fact. Yet to the Asian students in my class, there is perhaps more happening than is realized. Not completing the assignment well would all but destroy the relationship with their professor and university, devalue themselves in the eyes of their families and classmates, and seriously degrade the student's own self-worth. Every element of the process, from class attendance to reception of one's final grade, is an evaluative process by the whole community. Therefore, to the student inherently thinking in terms of HS, the price for public incompetence is far too high. Such shame inevitably echoes longer and further than thought possible.

Cultures tending toward honor and shame, then, deeply perceive how their actions will be perceived by those around them. Societal pressure is all-encompassing to live and act in specific ways. There is no such thing as a "lone ranger," striking out on his own path and assuming sole responsibility for his own actions. Yet by no means should such a mentality of "facework" be considered morally wrong; it is simply a fact of life. Indeed, it is quite healthy to consider how one's actions affect others. Flanders (2011) rightly comments, "To try to dispose of face would be akin to trying to eliminate DNA from human life, or the notion of the self from human thought. To be human is to have face and 'do' face, that is, engage in facework" (p. 84). To some extent, then, everyone plays this social game. It is therefore best to conclude that cultures cannot be sharply separated as individualist societies with IG thinking versus collectivist societies with HS. Better to view all cultures along a continuum between the two.

Yet where does Romania fall on the continuum? I will argue below that Romania tends toward the HS end of the spectrum. As mentioned above, this thesis will be viewed from several angles. First, however, a brief word concerning Romanian history is in order.

Romania at a Glance

The Eastern European nation of Romania is rapidly changing. Claiming descent from the ancient Romans, and even the Dacian tribe before, theirs is a culture that is continually caught between the Western appeal to modernism and the Eastern pull toward traditionalism. In the mid-1800s, nationalists succeeded in creating a united Romania under a constitutional monarchy that held out through the Second World War. At the conclusion of WWII, however, the Romanian Communist Party became strong enough to oust the king and establish socialist rule. Thus began Romania's forty years of Communism, nearly all of which were marked by dictatorial authority by the party leaders. When the winds of freedom began to blow through Eastern Europe in 1989, the tight grip of Romania's Communist leader, Nicolae Ceauşescu, finally was broken through bloody revolution. Now, 29 years later, Romania continues its path of self-discovery by wading through the wake of corruption left by the Communists and their successors.

History has not been kind to Romanians. Situated at the crossroads between Europe and Central Asia, much of Romanian history tells of wars with and between the Russians to the north and the Turks to the south. Aioanei (2006) posits, "Romania's greatest historical curse is that it is settled in a land of inevitable domination and permanent interference of contradictory internationally political streams" (p.707). For better or worse, such is Romania's story. Although this theme will be explored in detail below, suffice to say that Romania did make strides toward cultural pride after the establishment of the monarchy. Still, such steps forward were short-lived. Communist rule all but dismantled any civic pride cultivated in the years before WWII. Romanian historian Djuvara (2014) comments, "The most tragic consequence of that half-century was that it destroyed our *soul* . . . For a tarnished morality is more difficult to mend than old factories" (p. 342-343, emphasis his). Clearly, the question of where to look for hope is not easily answered. Hitchins (2014) convincingly declares that this question dominates and continues to plague Romanian history.

A word should also be given about how modern Romania is daily changing. Although Romanians consistently elected presidents who held second-tier Communist posts prior to 1989, the tides have now turned. [2] Each president, however, failed to truly attack

---

[2]The nation's first three presidents since the elections of 1991 are Ion Iliescu, 1991-1996; 2000-2004 (former Secretary of the Communist Party), Emil Constantinescu, 1996-2000 (former trade union leader), and Traian Basescu,

corruption at the higher echelons of society. But that is changing. In late 2014, Romanians elected a new president who is not part of the Bucharest political machine. Romanians who only recently considered their voice too soft to be heard are becoming bolder each day. Long-held Romanian values are being expressed and openly challenged as never before. To the astute observer, this is truly a significant time for Romania.

Having thus presented a brief introduction of Romania and its current state, I will now proceed to demonstrate several focal points in which HS discussions can help uncover cultural realities. Specifically, I will discuss how HS relates to the Romanian language, education patterns, the concept of trust-building, and Roma (gypsy) stereotypes. Finally, using personal interviews conducted with Romanians, I will then construct a skeletal outline of who might be considered an honorable and shameful Romanian and why.

HS focal points in Romania

1. Language

2004-2014 (naval captain before 1989, yet considered a second-tier member of the former Communist party). The current president, Klaus Iohannis, taught high school physics and was never a party member. Iohannis was elected in 2014.

No doubt language reveals much about a people group. The positive uses of words build philosophical concepts, beautiful prose, and elegant lyrics which convey an enigmatic description of a culture in full bloom. The negative ways words are utilized can tear apart souls, fire warlike passion, and woefully slam the ambitious back into their incipient state. Such are the power of words in any language, and such are the power of words in the Romantic language of Romanian.

Romanian is a beautiful language, with roots mainly in the Latin and Slavic tongues (Hitchins, 2014, p. 19). Unlike English, all Romanian verbs are conjugated depending on both context and who is speaking, primarily because the second-person singular and plural verbs can be used informally or formally. Unfortunately, this is not as easy as it sounds. The alert speaker must know precisely when is appropriate to address his audience in the formal or informal fashion. In short, the speaker must be aware of the status of the other party, be it ascribed (unearned) or achieved (earned). The second-person singular informal verbs are used when speaking with someone of the same age or younger (ascribed status), a similar education or political status or lower (achieved status), or whenever adults are addressing children or animals. The second-person plural verbs are used where these roles are reversed, namely when the addressee is older, holds a higher educational degree or political office than the speaker, or the speakers wish to maintain a respectful distance from one another. In this way, Romanians know instinctively when it is appropriate to show honor to others.

As an example, I turn to my first experience substitute teaching at the Bucharest Baptist Seminary. While most seminary students get along fine in English, a few of them could not follow an entire lesson and so I spoke in Romanian. Because several of the students were older than me, I chose to use the formal verb forms when speaking directly to them. Visibly surprised, these same students insisted on using the formal forms when addressing me. I realized later that it was because of my role as professor, even if only for the day and even if I was younger than they, which merited this reaction. I have since been told that some Romanian professors also teach using the formal with students, though it is rare and communicates that the professor wishes to further the power distance between teacher and student.

To analyze this situation a bit further, it is helpful to consider some of the findings of the cultural research group known as The Hofstede Center. Although several others are defined on their website, only the power distance and individualism value comparisons will be shown because of their importance to the HS discussion.

Figure 1. Value Orientations of the United States compared to Romania.

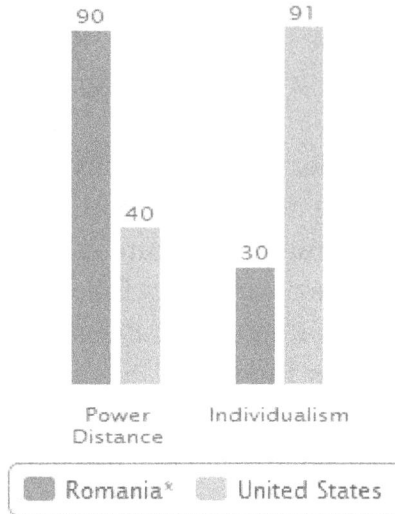

Source: The Hofstede Center. United States in comparison with Romania. Retrieved from http://geert-hofstede.com/united-states.html (accessed November 11, 2015).

Looking first at the value orientation of power distance, Romania scores exceptionally high compared to the United States. Power distance refers to the degree to which individuals and organizations accept differences in status, particularly from the view point of lower status members (Hofstede et. al., 2010). High power distance cultures accept inequality as unavoidable fact, whereas low power distance cultures prefer egalitarianism (p. 61). This means that Romanians are generally comfortable with the fact of inequality among societal members. Special recognition is shown to individuals who have attained higher education degrees, multiple titles and credentials, or elders. The Romanian language reinforces this mentality, with every verb denoting a specific conjugation for persons of higher status or age. Regular speech, then, perpetuates the role of power distance in the Romanian culture.

As we have seen, HS thinking relates to perceiving one's position as either threatened or heightened based on the actions of others. Romanians "save face" and show honor keenly through their linguistic interactions. Shame results when one's hierarchical status is not respected. Pulled in front of their peers, the culprit is then disgraced to the extent that the punishment fits the crime. More will be said of shaming tactics in a moment.

2. Education

The second area of exploration is the traditional style of Romanian education. Philosophers of education describe how one's system of teaching communicates as much, if not more, as the content material. Historically, Romanian education uses shame to enforce its norms. In the traditional Romanian classroom, learning is teacher-directed and based primarily on rote memory instead of analysis (Marga, 2002; Kállay, 2012; Ciobanu, 2012). Generally speaking, students know that their place is not to question the teacher's ideas, for that would be tantamount to rebellion. And rebelling against the system brings shame. Just as in the example above from my first experience at the seminary, it is clear that

Romanians tend to keep the status quo concerning status and role. Of course, there are exceptions to this statement, but not enough to be of any real consequence.

Whereas one will have to search thoroughly for multiple proverbs discussing honor, Romanian literature has produced several proverbs related to the use of shame. One frequent proverb reads as follows: *Ruşinea e mai dureroasă decât sabia.* "Shame is more painful than the sword." In other words, punishment via shame goes further and hurts longer than other forms. Such is the case both inside and outside the home. To illustrate this idea, I draw on two personal examples.

The first example regards the idea of shame-based teaching in the home (parent to child). Earlier this year, an American friend who has lived in Romania nearly 20 years led a music camp for Romanian children at a Baptist church in Bucharest. My friend, Susan, was quite impressed with how quickly the children learned the material and exhibited a genuine passion for music. Knowing that they were scheduled to perform a recital on the final day before all of their parents, Susan set aside a half-hour for the students to pray for the concert. One-by-one, each child prayed a similar prayer that included the words, "*Şi să nu ne fie ruşine.*" "And let us not be shamed." Fear of shaming themselves in front of their parents and community was obviously deeply embedded on the children's minds. To perform well would honor the parents. To perform poorly would shame all involved.

The second example is taken from a memory of my Romanian language teacher from before the fall of Communism. Although this scene took place roughly thirty years ago, it is noteworthy because remnants of public shaming in the public school system are still at play. My language teacher, Diana, recalls mornings before the start of the school day when each class would form lines in front of the main entrance. In front of the students stood the classroom teachers, all waiting for the appearance of the headmaster. When the headmaster arrived in front of the school, individual teachers would then call in front any student who had disobeyed them the previous day. The student's sins would then be read aloud for all to hear and punishment administered if necessary. While obviously serving to reign in any potential lawbreaker, Diana remembers how greatly shaken students became each time the scene was repeated.

The two examples given above indicate how authority figures use traditionally-accepted concepts of HS to educate children and young people. The honorable child will sing well because he is constantly aware that he and his parents will be shamed if he misses a note. The honorable child will strictly obey their teacher for fear of being publicly called out as a failure. In both cases, the general opinion of the group is most valuable. Conformity is king. Indeed, the whole socialist agenda is based on this idea of group identity.

It is no surprise, then, that cultures with a long past of wide scale socialism tend toward HS. Such cultures use the reality of public pressure to reward and punish socially-acceptable behavior.

It will be helpful here to pause briefly to mention that educating others in order to establish a sense of shame is by no means morally wrong. To affirm such a statement would be to negatively judge billions of the world's people, and this will simply not do. Remembering and acting on the reality of shame can be greatly beneficial as pertains to human behavior and interaction. DeSilva (1995) believes that a sense of shame is "indispensable for becoming a properly socialized part of one's society" (p. 62). For example, I choose not to drive in the wrong direction on one-way streets. Not only am I aware that it is illegal and there will be financial consequences, but I also should think about how many others could be affected by such a poor decision. The point is that, contrary to individualistic thinking, the entire group is involved in a transgression.

3. Trust-building

A third area of HS in Romanian culture concerns the building of another's trust. The relational nature of Latin cultures is not disputed, meaning that one must take time and effort to earn the esteemed title of friend. The most basic network that will result in favors in Romania is the family. Further, when a friend proves himself as trustworthy, he is then invited in as an "extended family member." How all of this relates to HS is in the area of reciprocity in the context of relationship. If a family member needs my money for food, it would be utterly shameful to watch them starve when I could have easily helped with that need. No matter that the family member in need is a distant cousin that I only see at weddings and things. A sense of HS ensures that help from family is on the way.

Reciprocity is evident at all levels of Romanian society. To their credit, most Romanians cannot imagine a world in which family and friends will not willingly inconvenience themselves to aid one another. For good or for ill, they are all connected as family. When asked to define the nuanced concept of "family," one Romanian friend interestingly declared:

> The purpose for which you live. The purpose for which you work. For us as Romanians, the family is an ideal, I can say. It cannot always be explained, meaning that at no time did I ever learn what 'family' actually means. It is a community of people who have the same interest even though they are different people, trying to find an equilibrium or balance to hold together a group and the interests of the group. Meaning that you develop and identify as a single group compared to the rest of the world as a family, as a name. For us as Romanians, family is very important, and this theme plays out in everything. So if you work, you work for

> the family. And if you do something extraordinary, you do it for the family. If you steal, because there are many people caught doing this, they declare that they did it for their family even if they have to sacrifice themselves. . . So it is a thing that for us as Romanians, family is everything.

It is easy to comprehend how this collectivist mindset relates to HS. Every opportunity for advancement, whether professionally or financially, is a chance to build up or tear down the honor of one's family. Often this is a good thing, such as when a dying parent is taken in to live with her children. Such reasoning can, however, also take dark forms. Public corruption is rampant in Romania because it is expected that friends do "favors" for friends, be it simply appointing an unqualified official or allowing a nightclub to function without the proper fire-safety paperwork. The cultural mores of HS demand that friendships be rewarded when needs must be met.

Building trust takes time in any culture, but especially in Romania. Again, this is not a bad thing; it is merely a fact of life. Compared to my own culture, however, the time taken to become part of one's trusted network seems incredibly long. Discussions of HS can aid the process, though, because Romanians inherently think in terms of hierarchy and reciprocity. If the natural hierarchy is not respected and terms are not met, it is no wonder that trust-building will take even more time than expected. Better to play by the rules of the social game, showing honor to who honor is due, and reciprocating personal favors when given. In this way, the system will be respected; not merely the intercultural system in play, but also the HS paradigm.

4. Roma Stereotypes

The fourth and final element that will be discussed in this paper relates to how Romanians view Roma (gypsy) culture. This concept is important for at least two reasons. First, Romanians are associated worldwide with Roma, due to the large percentage of Roma originally from Romania. Second, Romanians have historically discriminated against Roma as being racially inferior. The tendency for Romanians, then, is to distance themselves from this stereotype. These ideas will be briefly explained below, especially as they concern HS values.

Roma history is anything but pleasant. The Roma were most likely members of the Untouchable caste in northwestern India who began wandering westward and settling in groups in the Danube-Black Sea region of southeast Europe in the 14th century. Djuvara (2014) posits that the people group was "made up of people who had no land, no houses and no freedom of movement – in a word, slaves" (p. 100). It is well-documented that, for most of the time since, Romanian nobles legally enslaved the Roma. A multitude of popular Romanian fairy tales include portraits of Roma as uncouth, uneducated, and rotten (Mawr, 2008;

Kremnitz & Percival, 2010). Today, Romanian cities host thousands of Roma who earn their living as beggars and villages often include a poorer "Roma section." Yet by no means is this true of every ethnic Roma. Personally, I know many Roma people that I consider fortunate to count as friends. The above stereotypes, however, reinforce the idea for Romanians that the Roma are an inherently-shamed community.

To illustrate this concept, I take as an example a conversation with a Romanian bus driver roughly two years ago. My wife and I were conversing with him about what we liked and disliked about Romania, speaking fondly of the beauty of the Transylvanian mountains and the sunny seaside. As the dialogue transitioned to dislikes, the bus driver spat several choice words about the Roma. Upon seeing that we did not share his point of view, the bus driver began listing the many things wrong with Roma. One of these included that "they are here to serve *us*." Evidently, the bus driver's racism had a long memory. He was further shocked upon our relating that the next week we were to serve at a camp for Roma Christian youth. In the mind of our bus driver, any interaction with the Roma, especially living a whole week with them, was unthinkable. Obviously, this is an extreme example that I have only encountered verbally a few times, but it does serve to express how disgraceful Romanians may often view Roma.

Due to Romania's low economy, myriads of the most educated and hard-working Romanians emigrate each year to Western Europe, Canada, and the United States. Unfortunately, many of the native citizens of those countries know nothing of Romania except the large population of Roma. Romanian emigrants find that they must prove to their new neighbors that they are not, as Cher put it, "gypsies, tramps, and thieves." I have heard personal testimonies of Romanians lying about their ethnic origin because of the shame that could result, largely based on the association of Romania with Roma. The shameful stereotype is slowly shaken off through late hours at work and earning an honest living.

The four preceding characteristics, language, education, trust-building, and Roma stereotypes, assist in beginning the discussion of HS in Romania. Certainly these four characteristics are not an exhaustive list of HS in Romanian culture. If space allowed, more could easily be added. Yet now that several areas of HS have been briefly explored, it will be helpful to hear specific voices concerning how HS is indigenously perceived. Based on these personal testimonies, conclusions will then be drawn in discerning more precisely how Romanians define these realities.

5. Romanian Voices

Intrigued by the paradigm of HS, I interviewed five Romanians of various ages concerning who they might elect as an example of (1) an honorable Romanian, and (2) a shameful Romanian. Because the Romanian

Revolution of 1989 was as much a psychological revolution as it was a political one, I wanted to discover if differences exist between how HS is defined based on age group. One participant came of age under the Communist regime, two recall the crossover from Communism to democracy, and two are not old enough to have any recollection of Romanian socialism. The results were indeed fascinating, though not as diverse as expected, leading to the potential conclusion that it is possible to at least somewhat pinpoint an objective Romanian understanding of HS. All interviews were conducted entirely in Romanian and afterward transcribed into English. Findings from each interview will be quickly relayed.

The first interviewee is Samuel, age 45. Samuel was 18 years old during the revolution and has kindly spent several hours sharing stories with me about Bucharest in Communist days. His example of an honorable Romanian is General Ion Antonescu. Known primarily as the Romanian military leader who forced the king to abdicate and allied Romania with Nazi Germany, Antonescu is generally considered a dark dictator (Hitchins, 2014, p. 202-215). When asked why he chose Antonescu, Samuel declares that that he appreciates how Antonescu maintained his principles in the face of danger. Samuel admirably states, "Even though he knew that he would be thrown out and killed at some point, he decided to continue to sustain his concepts that what he did was better for Romania. And I think he was right in this" (personal communication, September 30, 2015). Conversely, Samuel's example of a shameful Romanian is Nicolae Ceaușescu, the Communist dictator who was overthrown in 1989. Interestingly, it is because Ceaușescu later went back on his word after having set out in a direction that would benefit the economy. Samuel again, "If you have your own conceptions and principles, go with them until the end, even if you have to sacrifice yourself. Ceaușescu did not do this." At least for Samuel, HS is tied directly to living out one's original principles.

The two people interviewed due to their experiences of Romania being both a Communist and democratic republic are Diana, age 33 and wife of Samuel, and Laurenția, age 29. Diana's example of an honorable Romanian is the Romanian king Stephen the Great, who successfully defended northeastern Romania from Ottoman advances for nearly 50 years (Hitchins, 2014, p. 29). Recounting her reasons for choosing Stephen the Great, Diana remarks, "But he was a dignified man, who never betrayed his country or his people and who worked toward a well-defined purpose." Concerning a shameful Romanian, Diana chose the first president of post-revolution Romania, Ion Iliescu. For Diana, it is the methods Iliescu used in taking power that make him shameful. "I consider all of the means by which he came to power to be shameful. People died in the Revolution without [Iliescu] caring . . . and he profited from the ignorance of the people and took power very easily through these means."

Strikingly similar are the remarks of Laurenția. Laurenția's honorable example is the professional tennis player Simona Halep, who currently holds several world titles. In Halep, Laurenția sees a patriotism that provides a positive face of Romania to the world. Laurenția smilingly states, "But Simona Halep is a person that works hard, is sincere, nice, and I liked this. I don't watch a lot of tennis but from what I observed, she transmits this value of pride for her people, for Romanians." On the other hand, Laurenția's shameful example is the prime minister, Victor Ponta, who is shameful because he holds such a high post but is incessantly caught up in scandals.[3]

It would seem, then, that both Diana and Laurenția believe that an honorable person does not betray their country and is successful in their profession using honest means. Both also agree that shame is rightly caused by dishonest gain and political scandal. There is thus a correlation between the testimonies of Diana and Laurenția.

The final two Romanians interviewed are Carmelia and Dragoș, ages 26 and 24 respectively. Carmelia's example of an honorable Romanian is her father, because even after he lost his business, he chose to remain in their village and find lesser paying

---

[3]Ponta would later be forced by the president to resign.

construction work. Carmelia contrasts this example with that of her friend's father, who also owned a construction company in the same village. When this other man's business collapsed, however, he "renounced his family and left the country, and even today they have no connection with him. For me, these are things that are essential in how you view the honor of a person. Because he ran from his responsibilities and didn't face the consequences for his actions."

Dragoş did not draw from personal experience in answering the HS questions. Dragoş's example of an honorable Romanian is Protestant pastor Richard Wurmbrand. Dragoş's words, chock full of HS value language, are worth repeating here at length:

> Richard Wurmbrand, who was courageous in his position as a Christian in the face of persecution. Even if he is not necessarily known for his values in that period, his values were seen in time based on the decisions he made. So his decisions even in a time of chaos because of what he believed and courage is the absence of shame. He displayed some healthy values. So for me to display healthy values – to love those around you, to be selfless, **to be giving, sincere** (emphasis mine).

Dragoş also chose Prime Minister Victor Ponta as his example of a shameful Romanian, for much the same reasons Laurenţia gave above in her evaluation.

141

Based on the interviews with Carmelia and Dragoș, younger Romanians see a clear correspondence between HS and bravely fighting for one's values. Renunciation of family for greater fortune or higher political status, especially if that entails leaving the country, is not seen as honorable. This reality is so widespread that whole generations mature under the care of grandparents, because one's parents have left the country to find work elsewhere. Not always are parents' reasons immoral, nor do they wish to leave their children countries apart, but it is interesting to hear that Romanians generally do not find this choice to be honorable. Selflessness is the honorable route, though often choices like these are not so black and white.

Several comments can be made in assessing similarities between the five interviews. First, honor is bestowed upon those who maintain their principles. Even if one's values are wrong, better to follow through with one's plans and receive honor than shift directions midstream and bear shame. Second, the honorable Romanian does not run from adversity. Each example expressed that, even if death is a possibility, a man or woman will have honor if they do not cripple under impending conflict. Third, the methods one uses in attaining power matter more than status achieved. Every example given displays how Romanians remember well how their heroes and villains climbed the ladders of power. Fourth, Romanians do not believe honor is to be found in politics. Romanian news gives examples *ad nauseum* of politicians caught red-handed in political corruption, leading to the belief that no one of the political class is clean. Fifth, Romanians render multiple more examples of shameful people than honorable. Upon being asked an example of a shameful Romanian, every person interviewed either began by laughing, joking by asking how long we have to talk, or exclaiming how easy it is to find such an example. These characteristics, added to the findings found in the preceding sections of this analysis, move closer to attaining an objective definition of HS ideology in Romania.

Conclusion

The preceding study attempts to expose elements of HS in Romanian culture. Due to its geographical placement in Europe, Romania is generally not considered a location where HS is a visible reality. Further, many cross-cultural commentators hail from the Global West and therefore tend towards a different paradigm of thought and value processing (innocence-guilt, or IG). Reflection on Romanian culture, then, will often look and feel out of place. Conclusions drawn in this paper are meant to counter this tendency.

As opposed to IG, the HS system calculates the perspective of the collective before taking action. This tends to be the case in Romania. One's choices will inevitably affect the group around them. Such groupthink is burned so deeply into the worldview that individual preferences become obsolete. For the person in the world of HS, everything one does is a conversation in whether or not it will project an honorable face to the community. Yet the alternative, which brings shame to the community, must be avoided at all costs.

In Romania, the HS game is played out at all times. From addressing one's boss at work to interacting with the street beggar while exiting the tram, there is always a culturally correct way to assert status and bestow the currency of honor. When one does not play by the rules well, the result is shame.

To return to the opening illustration of this essay, the Romanian footballers found themselves in the second half of their match floundering one to zero behind a team they should have long left in the dust. When all seemed lost, fans began booing and hissing at the Romanian players. To this American from an IG worldview, the scene happening around me was incomprehensible. Yet to a Romanian thinking in HS terms, the team needed the boost that only shaming could give. After all, *"Ruşinea e mai dureroasă decât sabia"* ("Shame is more painful than the sword").

CHAPTER SEVEN:

TOWARDS A SUSTAINABLE MENTORING
MODEL IN THE ROMANIAN BIBLE
COLLEGE[1]

Once there was a professor named David. Although I had known David for several years and taken classes with him, our relationship changed immediately following a personal heartbreaking crisis. In a moment of sheer desperation, David actively listened as I poured out my heart. I began to meet regularly with David, sometimes even twice per week, both inside and outside his office. Only a few short months from graduating college, David moved beyond the role of professor and even that of friend. Opening the Bible, his home, and his family to me, David gave me inestimable advice that I genuinely saw lived out before my eyes. Again, David was not simply a professor. David was a cherished mentor with whom I still keep in touch.

Mentoring is a difficult concept to define. Several sources offer multiple definitions, each

---

[1]This essay was first presented at the 2017 Southeast Regional Conference of the Evangelical Missiological Society (Wake Forest, NC), and then again at the 2017 National Conference of the Evangelical Missiological Society (Dallas, TX).

providing a nuanced view that may be either quite simplistic or complicated (Crutcher, 2007; Goetsch & Rasmussen, 2008). More recently, authors affirm a sharp distinction between formal and informal mentoring, especially in ecclesiastic contexts (Dever, 2016; Reid & Robinson, 2016). For clarity's sake, however, I will define mentoring as purposefully assisting someone with lesser experience in a particular area of life and/or work in order that they may better meet the coming challenges. More difficult still is the implementation of multiple mentoring relationships.

The following pages include the beginnings of a teaching plan that aims to introduce the concept of mentoring at the Romanian Bible college in which I teach. I begin first by briefly defining the learners and context, specifically developing the concept of "high power distance culture." Several cultural challenges to mentoring are then delineated. Afterward, I conclude by proposing a transferrable mentoring model for similar Bible colleges in the Majority World.

Learners and Context

The Romanian Baptist seminary, formally called the *Institutul Teologic Baptist Bucureşti*, is the oldest of Romania's Baptist seminaries. Founded in 1921 in collaboration with the Southern Baptist Convention's International Mission Board, of which I am a missionary, the seminary is proud of its heritage of producing many of the nation's leading Baptist pastors.

Although called a seminary, the institution is more of a Bible college than a graduate school, with the majority of pastoral theology students ranging between 18-25 years of age.

Besides myself and another missionary from the US, the multiple professors are all Romanian Baptist pastors. There are a few Romanian professors in their 30s and 40s, yet the majority are all age 50 and above. The other professors are incredibly kind men, having served for many years as pastors of local churches in Bucharest and other cities. To teach at the college, one must have at least been in ministry for several years and obtained a master's degree. Each of these qualifications will become apparent below as not only job qualifications, but also as deeply-held cultural values that define the type of person that may be allowed to teach in a Romanian Baptist college. Let me illustrate with a personal story.

Shuffling to our seats in the well-lit congregation of the elaborately decorated Baptist church pastored by the seminary president, I adjust my tie because I know soon my name will be called in recognition as a professor and missionary. This is the official convocation service for the new school year, and everyone is dressed in shining suits and ties. On the raised platform of the pulpit stand the seminary president and his cabinet, flanked by the raised stadium seating of the seminary students in matching suits on one side and the church orchestra on the other. Seated in the row above the students are the seminary's full-time professors, also in matching suits. Glancing at my wife, I whisper that we are in for a long evening. Institution history, sermons, and special music performances are delivered by men with multiple titles and letters following their names. Each professor and visiting official must be acknowledged, and overall it is a joyful service. As we are leaving, I am delighted that my students from last year all manage to find me to say hello.

It is for the men on the raised platform that the following introduction to mentoring is intended. Ideally, the setting might be a sort of "faculty meeting" in the seminary chapel room, where we may all gather together as brothers and discuss the realities and possibilities of mentoring our students to be better equipped for real-life ministry. These are valiant men who have served tirelessly for decades, often receiving meager salaries from their churches and their teaching posts. These are educated men who have received master and doctoral degrees from both the University of Bucharest and prestigious institutions in the United States and United Kingdom. These are encouraging men who faithfully preach God's truth and long to see more churches planted and more Romanians saved. These are good men. I have seen, however, that a gap exists. Although mentoring future leaders is a noted goal in theory, both current students and pastor friends tell me that this is not happening. I believe that bringing the matter to the attention of these professors is the logical first step. Yet before outlining my lesson plan, I will relate several cultural challenges to the mentoring task that must be addressed.

Cultural Challenges

The Eastern European nation of Romania is a land filled with diversity. Vacillating between an urban modernity modeled after the Global West and the rural conservatism owing to roots looking eastward, the verdict is still out concerning what sort of shape post-Communist Romania will take (Hitchins, 2014). Wave after wave of foreign conquerors tempted by the outlet of the Danube Delta have caused Romanian soil to serve as a battleground for centuries. The tumultuous history of Romania demonstrates, for many Romanians, the inescapable reality that power structures are unavoidable and one must always remember precisely where he or she stands in the social ladder. Political historian Tom Gallagher (2005) explains:

> Romanians have been viewed as subjects rather than citizens by successive regimes of contrasting political hues. There is no doubt that the legacy of vertical dependence and exploitation inherited from foreign rule . . . cast a long shadow over the independent Romanian state.

For better or worse, such is the Romanian story.

Vertical dependence and power structures are seen in multiple segments of Romanian society. These realities are exceptionally apparent, however, in the Romanian classroom (Armstrong, 2015). Professors and students know their place well, and everything from classroom vocabulary of respect to seating arrangements reflects this trend. Such tendencies maintain a level of power distance that is socially acceptable. For example, the Romanian language is composed with verbs that use both formal and informal forms. Students always use the formal verb case when addressing professors. When professors use the formal verb case with students, however, there is a visible confusion in students' faces. As a cultural outsider, I have encountered this cultural oddity numerous times in my teaching when wanting to address a student who is clearly older than me but is momentarily shaken by my use of the formal forms of address. Power distance must be considered in the Romanian classroom.

Mentoring, by its very nature, involves two parties with differing experience levels drawing closer to one another. The closer into one's life the mentor allows his mentee to enter, the deeper the mentoring experience. Clearly, such mention of close proximity could defy the maintenance of power distance, though not necessarily so. Reid & Robinson believe there are at least two types of mentoring: formal and informal. In formal mentoring, leaders meet regularly with one or more individuals for accountability and teaching. Conversely, informal mentoring brings mentees into the mentor's daily life. Whereas formal mentoring is easier to schedule, it is also easier to pretend that life is "all good." Informally mentoring someone involves the mentor taking their people with them in normal daily activities, such as going to a basketball game or grabbing a quick breakfast before class. Reid & Robinson (2016) helpfully write that this second type of mentoring is more effective in the long run because mentees experience firsthand how their mentors deal with challenges such as time, family, and profession (Kindle Location 262).

In the following introductory lesson plan, I will make a case that Romanian Bible college professors employ a mentoring model. After developing each section, I offer a fuller description of the mixed formal and informal mentoring model. The model is formal in the sense that it is structured and requested by the institution. The mentoring program will be added onto the tasks of student church practicums that must be completed each semester. Yet the model is also informal in the sense that professors are encouraged to invite students into their offices and homes in order to better glimpse the life of a pastor-scholar. Along the way, I will offer several insights gleaned from personal interviews conducted with seminary graduates who are now pastors in Bucharest.

Mentoring Plan Development

Each segment of the mentoring plan is hereafter developed, albeit in a briefer and perhaps more structured sense than would be the case in the classroom setting. Again, the ideal setting is a faculty meeting among professors, all of whom are Baptist pastors that have served faithfully for a number of years. Although the target audience is, of course, the Romanian evangelical college, professors in other cultures will recognize similarities in their contexts.

I.   Introduction

The lesson begins with my thanking the professors in general, and the president in particular, for the opportunity to share with them about mentoring. Their years of professional and pastoral experience deserve recognition, thereby affirming their status as more advanced in experience than I.

To introduce the concept of mentoring, stories such as that of my professor-mentor named David, which I relayed at the beginning of this inquiry, provide a powerful point of entry. Emphasis should be placed on the fact that Professor David brought me into his life, introducing me to his family and opening his home. From Professor David I learned that there is more to being a professor than possessing several degrees. The transparent heart of a Christian teacher for the true welfare of one's students longs to see them thrive in all areas of life.

II.   Jesus as Mentor

Although I by no means wish to lecture the professors before me, I do want to first point them to at least one biblical reference. In Mark 3:14, readers are told that, "[Jesus] appointed twelve so that they might be with him, and that he might send them out to preach." Jesus' principal method of discipling, then, was time spent together. The disciples spent time with Jesus in both formal teaching locations, such as synagogues, and informal settings, such as walking along the roadside. Jesus shared laughter, stories, meals, and even finances with his disciples. They watched closely how Jesus reacted in diverse situations.

At this point, I will divide the professors before me into pairs. Each pair must respond to the following question: What were some specific ways in which Jesus mentored his disciples? Answers will vary, but the following is a potential list:

- Stories
- Sermons
- Parables
- Personal/Real life illustrations
- One-on-one conversation
- Group discussion
- Empowering the disciples to assist him

The desire at this point is to affirm the professors' superior knowledge and status, as well as push them to consider the diverse ways that Jesus mentored others. Each pair should be given the opportunity to share their ideas and explain their answers. Although I do not want to belabor the point, Jesus' goal clearly went beyond teaching to equipping the disciples for a similar type of ministry in their future.

III.	One thing I wish I'd learned in seminary is...

Due to the personal nature of pastoral ministry, in the sense that it is a people-focused profession, seminary students would do well to see and hear firsthand accounts of how seasoned pastors overcome struggles. Every ministry leader has days in which they look back and quip, "Seminary never prepared me for that." I argue that this does not always have to be the case.

As an example, I return to my mentor, David. While undergoing a particularly difficult period of deciding what to do with my future due to an unforeseen breakup, I remember feeling emotionally and physically spent. Collapsing into an armchair in David's office, my eyes began tearing up as I recounted how I had hinged so many plans on that relationship progressing. Two months from graduating college with a degree in history education, my dream as a local high school history teacher was fading fast. I will never forget two things from that day: the genuine compassion for my soul in David's eyes and the determination in his voice that life can move on. Then David spoke these two sentences that I still return to a decade later: "You are young and bright and single. If you want to teach in the US Virgin Islands, teach in the

US Virgin Islands." One month later I applied and landed a history teacher position on the little island of Saipan in the Northern Mariana Islands.

Four years later, I took seminary classes on counseling. But I could never have learned from a book how to counsel a heartbroken college student like myself. Many lessons are like that.

Thus I return to the professors before me and ask, "What is one thing about ministry you wish you'd learned in seminary?" Each pair will be given ample time to discuss and present their findings. Answers may include the following:

- Comfort a dying church member
- Counsel someone dealing with addiction (drugs, alcohol, pornography, etc.)
- How to hire/fire church staff
- Managing a church budget
- Convening a prayer meeting
- Preparing for special services (baby dedication, baptism, wedding, funeral, retreats)
- Balancing family and ministry
  Most likely, group discussion will begin at this point. This is healthy, but should not be allowed to overwhelm the time.

IV.   Proposal of Mentoring Model

After having looked at multiple ways in which Jesus mentored others and several areas of ministry in which we all found ourselves ill-equipped, hopefully the tone will be set for action steps. Before I begin discussing individual mentoring stages, I want to be clear that the following model utilizes the student practicum program already in place. As in other Majority World theological institutions, every pastoral theology student at the Bucharest seminary is required to complete several practica each year in Romanian Baptist churches. During holiday breaks, such as Christmas and Easter, students are usually sent to minister in small churches around the country. During the regular semester, however, students are assigned a church in Bucharest in which to serve. One pastor with whom I spoke, who I will call Pastor T, mentioned that there is an unspoken expectation that mentoring will happen between the pastor and seminary student. Further, another pastor, Pastor A, notes that there is a lack of "concrete interest" in mentoring. A third pastor, Pastor G, confided that because a system of accountability is not in place, many students assigned to specific churches tend to "church hop" from one Bucharest church to another. Church pastors, therefore, are not able to become personally invested in the students.

What I am proposing, then, is that the professors that serve as pastors in the churches where students are sent for practicum follow the mentoring model below. In this way, nothing need necessarily change concerning the sending of students to serve in churches. The following model is merely a system to provide accountable mentoring at the base level, thereby placing the least amount of pressure on both mentor and mentee.

Often when I talk with my students about what they did during their practica, I usually receive the following response: "I preached a sermon or two." By no means am I saying that asking students to fill one's pulpit is not good. On the contrary, this provides valuable experience for the developing pastor-to-be. Yet if this is all that constitutes a practicum, and there is little actual time spent with the pastor and staff, I would argue that such a practicum is not as enriching and rewarding as possible. In such a case, there is no difference between the one-time visiting preacher and the seminary student assigned to a pastor for practicum.

At the crux of the mentoring model I am proposing here are one-on-one conversations and a corresponding activity. Pastor-professors sit down and talk with students individually at least once per month. To reiterate, students are assigned a different Bucharest church each semester, meaning roughly three or four conversations maximum. One activity for each semester is given. Each year is broken down by theme, and the themes are intended to guide these conversations so that the seminary student is better aware of how pastors approach these large issues. Each year's theme will be developed below.

Year One: The Pastor as Scholar.

First-year students serving practica in professors' churches talk through their studies and the importance of loving God through efficient scholarship. I have intentionally placed the theme of "pastor as scholar" for the first year in order that students might begin their theological studies properly. Students must be reminded that excellent work from God's people imitates the excellent work of God himself.

In the course of my conversation with my friend, Pastor G, there was a recurring theme that Romanian evangelical leaders often do not promote good scholarship. It is unfortunate that this is the case, and in many ways indicative of the larger evangelical world. As historian Mark Noll (1994) eloquently demonstrates in *The Scandal of the Evangelical mind,* an emphasis on studies and developing reason wrongly appears to place evangelicals at odds with faith. Therefore, there is largely a wholesale abandonment of teaching the next generation to love God with one's mind.

Pastors who serve as mentors for Bible college students have the power to change this misperception. Mentors should take time to talk through issues of loving God as diligent students of God's word. Only one of the four pastors I spoke with mentioned that their Romanian professors pushed them to excel at their studies. Granted, students will have differing levels of aptitude for long hours spent reading and writing. Nevertheless, the cultivation of a pastor's mind plays a significant role in their calling. Speaking from personal experience as a professor, there are quite a few students who are satisfied with merely passing grades, unwilling to take the extra step to obtain maximum points. I believe if students found that their professors were truly interested in their academic pursuits, grades would improve and self-confidence could be lifted.

The semester activity, then, asks the professor-mentor to invite students into his personal office where they do their deepest study. Conversations that take place in the heart of a pastor's office, surrounded perhaps by sermon notes and biblical commentaries, serve as positive reinforcement that pastors ought to take their studies seriously. Personally, I do not take it lightly when a professor invites me into his office to discuss academic issues one-on-one.

Year Two: The Pastor as Disciple.

Although pastors are constantly giving of themselves through public and personal communication and presence, the wise pastor is humble enough to know that each day they need Christ's refilling. How easy it is to overload a daily schedule with talking about God and never stopping to be with God. The temptations for ministers to run to and fro lead a disproportionate majority to sin, burnout, and depression, and seminary students must hear of such realities.

Still another Romanian pastor, Pastor R, nostalgically recalled how a professor who informally mentored him during his student years never began a class without personal time in prayer. Pastor R watched closely during these moments, vividly remembering them even after 20 years. Clearly this professor lived and mentored out of his personal walk with the Lord.

Speaking with others about a personal relationship with Christ, and especially with one's students, will not come naturally. Comparatively, it is easier to stand in front of a large crowd and expound a text of Scripture than to speak openly about the daily practice and desire of devotional time with God. Even confessing that days sometimes go by without such daily times helps in showing students that their mentors are also human and encounter struggles. Mentors must have the courage to pastor students in this way, however, because they very well may be retelling those memories, like Pastor R, 20 years later. Thus, the activity requested of the pastor is to invite students in one morning for their daily time with the Lord.

Year Three: The Pastor as Family Man.

The sad reality of overworked and depressed pastors often ends in shipwrecked marriages. It is as if pastors believe that busy-ness is next to godliness, and often the greatest casualty is the family (Boyd, 2014). In a fast-moving city like Bucharest, moreover, time is a precious commodity and time home with family is a battle for which pastors must fight. Seminary students would do well to know this from their student years, especially as they prepare to marry.

During my own seminary days, the pastors and leaders of my church placed an abundant focus on the cultivation of joyful homes. The wives and children of these men were wonderful people to be around. Even before that time, while sitting in my mentor David's home or talking with his family over dinner or the occasional backyard campfire, I loved seeing how the whole family embraced my mentor's role of hosting university students. And I longed to do the same for others if God ever blessed me with a family.

As a professor now, my wife and I host my class at least once per semester in our home. We usually prepare some sort of finger food and coffee or tea and have relaxed conversation with the students. I recognize that such a practice may decrease the level of power distance and, potentially, respect, but this has not been an issue in our case. I want my seminary students to see how I interact with my wife and daughter. I want them to see how I allow my wife to initiate conversation and how I serve her and wash her and my students' dishes. I want them to see how love permeates our home in everything from the pictures we've chosen for the walls to the large print Bible verse that hangs above our television. The activity for third year students asks professors to do the same for the students serving practicums in their churches.

Year Four: The Pastor as Shepherd. In many ways, crafting and preaching sermons well can be largely learned from books (Akin, Allen, & Matthews, 2010; .Richard, 2001). This is not the case with learning to pastor well, because pastoring by its very nature calls for apprenticeship, humility, and a genuine love for intrapersonal relationships (Baxter, 2011; Croft, 2015). Pastoring involves fallibly communicating the divine love of God to fallible people whom God loves. In the words of John Piper (2013), pastoring well is recognition that "we are not professionals."

As the students' four year Bible college journey draws to a close, by this point in their academic pursuit they will hopefully better understand theology and some practical theology. Building upon this foundation, allowing mentees to then view the practical aspects of one's ministry makes sense. Specifically, young pastors find themselves ill-equipped for the areas of pastoral ministry that do not involve preaching, such as personal evangelism, counseling, and the coordinating of administrative tasks. Bringing fourth-year Bible college students into conversations about how pastors meet these challenges would be highly beneficial, especially since a number of the new graduates move right into pastoral ministry upon graduation.

Mentoring conversations at this stage center around the practicalities of church dynamics, whereas previous years are perhaps further removed and theoretical. In other words, this final stage of the mentoring program might be nicknamed the "nuts and bolts" phase, due to its intensely practical focus.

Mentees ask questions and see firsthand how pastors prepare for special services, such as baptisms, funerals, and financial management.

A possible representation for the mentoring model is that of a church building with four pillars. Built on the solid foundation of Scripture and directed upward for the glory of God, each pillar is made up of the mentoring theme for each year of Bible college: scholar, disciple, family man, and shepherd. It is my contention that the firm upholding of these pillars will go a long way in preserving a well-rooted and lasting ministry.

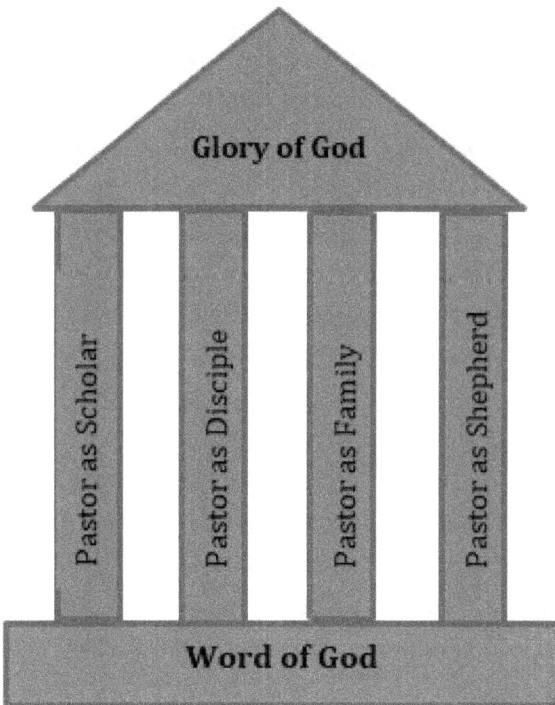

Glory of God

Pastor as Scholar

Pastor as Disciple

Pastor as Family

Pastor as Shepherd

Word of God

Conclusion

In every era, missionaries wonder what will be their true legacy from the field. To establish a sustainable mentoring program in worldwide Bible colleges is a worthy, long-term goal. I believe that transferring this model to other Bible college contexts is possible. Of course, each culture and institution must contextualize the model to fit their needs. Contextualization questions will inevitably arise, such as:

1. **What does a contextually-appropriate method of accountability look like for students? For professors?**
2. **Is success considered by following the mentoring model exactly?**
3. **What is a reasonable time frame for implementation?**
4. **What about online students?**
5. **What about primarily and secondary oral contexts?**

Yet I contend that the mentoring model could function well if the change agents follow a similar procedure to the plan discussed above. In high power distance cultures, such as Romania, status and role among professors must be respected and affirmed. The future health of the church in Majority World regions depends upon rightly trained pastors who are both doctrinally and personally sound. Such sustainability that will long outlive us is what we are after. I am thankful for mentors who pushed me and brought me into real life ministry. As such, I desire no less for my own students in Romania.

<u>REFERENCES:</u>

Introduction:

Chapter One:

Adams, R. N. (1975). *Energy and structure: A theory of social power*. Austin: Univ. of Texas Press.

Aioanei, I. (2006). Leadership in Romania. *Journal of Organizational Change Management, 19*(6), 705-712.

Apeh, J. (1989). *Social Structure and church planting*. Atascadero, CA: Indigenous Missions International.

Djuvara, N. (2014). *A brief illustrated history of Romanians*. Bucharest, Romania: Humanitas.

Hofstede, G., Hofstede, G. J., & Minkov, M. (2010). *Cultures and organizations: Software of the mind*. New York: McGraw-Hill.

National Institute of Statistics Romania. (2013). *What does the 2011 census tell us about religion?* Bucharest, Romania: National Institute of Statistics Romania.

Lingenfelter, S. (1996). *Agents of transformation*. Grand Rapids: Baker.

Redfield, R. (1989). *The Little community, and peasant society and culture*. Chicago: Univ. of Chicago Press.

Rosen, L. (1984). *Bargaining for reality*. Chicago: Univ. of Chicago Press.

Schusky, E. (1983). *Manual for kinship analysis*. 2nd
    Edition. Lanham, MD: Univ. Press
    of America.

Chapter Two:
Adams, R. N. (1975). *Energy and structure: A theory
    of social power*. Austin: Univ. of Texas Press.
Aioanei, I. (2006). Leadership in Romania. *Journal of
    Organizational Change Management, 19*(6),
    705-712.
Bolman, L. G., & Deal, T. E. (2003). *Reframing
    organizations*. San Francisco, CA: Jossey-Bass.
Constantin, T., Pop D., & Stoica-Constantin, A.
    (2006). Romanian managers and human
resource management. *Journal of Organizational
    Change and Management, 19*(6), 760-765.
Djuvara, N. (2014). *A brief illustrated history of
    Romanians*. Bucharest, Romania: Humanitas.
Fein, E. C., Tziner, A., & Vasiliu, C. (2010). Age cohort
    effects, gender, and Romanian leadership
    preferences. *Journal of Management
    Development, 29*(4), 364-376.
Hammett, J. S. (2005). *Biblical foundations for
    Baptist churches: A contemporary
    ecclesiology.*
Grand Rapids, MI: Kregel.
Lingenfelter, S. (1998). *Transforming culture: A
    challenge for Christian mission* (2nd ed.).
Grand Rapids, MI: Baker.

Șerban, S. 2007. Institution development and corruption in local society in southeastern Europe. In K. Roth (Ed.), *Social networks and social trust in the transformation countries: Ethnological and Sociological Studies* (pp. 175-196). Zurich, Switzerland: Gimbl & Co.

Sikor, T., Stahl, J., & Dorondel, S. (2008). Negotiating property and state: Post-socialist struggles over Albanian and Romanian forests. Working paper 9. (pp. 1-26). Norwich, United Kingdom: The School of Development Studies, Univ. of East Anglia.

Uniunea Bisericilor Creştine Baptiste din România. (2008). "Statutul de organizare şi funcţionare a Cultul Creştin Baptist." Retrieved from http://uniuneabaptista.ro/rubenword/wp-content/uploads/2011/10/Statut.pdf.

Verdery, K. (2002). Seeing like a mayor: Or, how local officials obstructed Romanian land restitution. *Ethnography, 3*(1), 5-33.

Chapter Three:

Aioanei, I. (2006). Leadership in Romania. *Journal of Organizational Change Management, 19*(6), 705-712.

Arfire, R. (2011). The Moral regulation of the second Europe: Transition, Europeanization and the Romanians. *Critical Sociology, 37*(6), 853–870. doi:10.1177/0896920510398017

Coupland, N. (2008). The delicate constitution of identity in face-to-face accommodation: A response to Trudgill. *Language in Society 37*(2), 267-270.

Djuvara, N. (2014). *A brief illustrated history of Romanians*. Bucharest, Romania: Humanitas.

Dutu, C. B. (2004). A transatlantic "romance" in Romania. *Irish Journal of American Studies, 13/14*, 139–148.

Hofstede, G., Hofstede, G. J., & Minkov, M. (2010). *Cultures and organizations: Software of the mind*. New York: McGraw-Hill.

Ting-Toomey, S. (2005). Identity negotiation theory: Crossing cultural boundaries. In W. B. Gudykunst (ed.), *Theorizing about intercultural communication* (pp. 211-233). Thousand Oaks, CA: Sage.

Salacuse, J. W. (2010). "Teaching international business negotiation: Reflections on three decades of experience." *International Negotiation, 15*(1), 187-228.

Ting-Toomey, S., & Oetzel, J. G. (2001). *Managing intercultural conflict effectively*. Thousand Oaks, Calif: SAGE Publications.

Volf, M. (1995). "A vision of embrace: Theological perspectives on cultural identity and conflict." *The Ecumenical Review, 47*(2), 195-205.

Chapter Four:

Lovejoy, G. (2012). The extent of orality: 2012 update. *Orality Journal 1*(1): 29.

Chapter Five:

Harrison, L. E. & Huntington, S. P. (2000). *Culture matters: How values shape human progress.* New York, NY: Basic Books.

Hitchins, K. (2014). *A concise history of Romania.* Cambridge, UK: Cambridge Univ. Press.

Letham, R. (2007). *Through western eyes: Eastern Orthodoxy, a reformed perspective.* Geanies House, Great Britain: Christian Focus Publications, Ltd.

Litfin, D. (2012). *Word versus deed: Resetting the scales to a biblical balance.* Wheaton, IL: Crossway.

National Institute of Statistics Romania. (2013). What does the 2011 census tell us about religion in Romania? Bucharest, Romania: National Institute of Statistics Romania.

Pew Research Center. (2017, May 10). Religious belief and national belonging in central and eastern Europe. Retrieved May 24, 2017, from http://www.pewforum.org/2017/05/10/religious-belief-and-national-belonging-in-central-and-eastern-europe/.

Spann, M. (2001). *Witnessing to people of Eastern Orthodox background: Turning barriers of Belief into bridges to personal faith.* PhD diss. Southwestern Baptist Theological

Seminary, Fort Worth, TX.

St. Athanasius Orthodox Academy. (1993). *The Orthodox study Bible*. Nashville, TN: Thomas Nelson.

Van de Poll, E. & Appleton, J. (2015). *Church planting in Europe: Connecting to society, learning from experience*. Eugene, OR: Wipf & Stock.

Chapter Six:

Aioanei, I. (2006). Leadership in Romania. *Journal of Organizational Change Management, 19*(6), 705-712.

Ciobanu, L. (2012). Do Romanian schools produce idiots?. The Economist. Retrieved from http://www.economist.com/blogs/easternappr oaches /2012/08/education-romania.

DeSilva, D. A. (1995). *Despising shame: Honor discourse and community maintenance in the epistle to the Hebrews*. Atlanta, GA: Scholars Press.

Djuvara, N. (2014). *A brief illustrated history of Romanians*. Bucharest, Romania: Humanitas.

Flanders, C. L. (2011). *About face: Rethinking face for 21st century mission*. Eugene, OR: Wipf and Stock Publishers.

Hitchins, K. (2014). *A concise history of Romania*. Cambridge, UK: Cambridge Univ. Press.

Hofstede, G., Hofstede, G. J., & Minkov, M. (2010). *Cultures and organizations: Software of the mind.* New York: McGraw-Hill.

Kállay, É. (2012). Learning strategies and metacognitive awareness as predictors of academic achievement in a sample of Romanian second-year students. *Cognitie, Creier, Comportament/Cognition, Brain, Behavior, 16*(3), 369–385.

Kremnitz, M. & Percival, J. M. (2010). *Legends and folklore: Eighteen fairy tales from Romania.* Cedar Lake, MI: ReadaClassic.com.

Livermore, D. A. (2009). *Cultural intelligence: Improving your CQ to engage our multicultural world.* Grand Rapids: Baker.

Marga, A. (2002). Reform of education in Romania in the 1990s: A retrospective. *Higher Education in Europe, 27*(1/2), 123–135.

Mawr, E. B. (2008). *Romanian fairy tales and legends.* Charleston, SC: Forgotten Books.

Richards, E. R. & O'Brien, B. J. (2012). *Misreading Scripture with western eyes: Removing cultural blinders to better understand the Bible.* Downers Grove, IL: InterVarsity Press.

Wu, J. (2012). *Saving God's face: A Chinese contextualization of salvation through honor and shame.* Pasadena, CA: WCIU Press.

Chapter Seven:

Akin, D., Allen, D. L., & Matthews, N. (2010). *Text-driven preaching: God's word at the heart of every sermon*. Nashville, TN: B & H Academic.

Armstrong, C. D. (2015). Honor and shame cross-currents in Romanian culture. *Jurnal Teologic 14*(2): 95-123.

Baxter, R. (2011). *The reformed pastor*. CreateSpace Independent Publishing Group.

Boyd, B. (2014). *Addicted to busy*. Colorado Springs, CO: David C. Cook.

Croft, B. (2015). *The pastor's ministry: Biblical priorities for faithful shepherds*. Grand Rapids, MI: Zondervan.

Crutcher, B. N. (2007). Mentoring across cultures. *Academe 93*(4): 44-48.

Dever, M. (2016). *Discipling: How to help others follow Jesus*. Wheaton, IL: Crossway.

Gallagher, T. (2005). *Modern Romania: The end of Communism, the failure of democratic reform, and the theft of a nation*. New York: NYU Press.

Goetsch, J. & Rasmussen, M. (2008). *Mentoring and modeling: Developing the next generation*. Lancaster, CA: Striving Together Publications.

Hitchins, K. (2014). *A concise history of Romania*. Cambridge, UK: Cambridge Univ. Press.

Noll, M. (1994). *The scandal of the evangelical mind*. Grand Rapids, MI: Eerdmans.

Piper, J. (2013). *Brothers, we are not professionals: A plea to pastors for radical ministry.* Nashville, TN: B & H Publishing Group.

Reid, A. L. & Robinson, G. G. (2016). *With: A Practical Guide to Informal Mentoring and Intentional Disciple Making.* Nashville, TN: Rainer Publishing.

Richard, R. (2001). *Preparing expository sermons: A seven-step method for biblical preaching.* Grand Rapids, MI: Baker.

ABOUT THE AUTHOR

Cameron D. Armstrong works in church planting and theological education with the International Mission Board and is currently a PhD Intercultural Education candidate at Biola University. **Cameron lives in** Bucharest, Romania, with his wife, Jessica, and their two children, Sara and Noah. Cameron can be reached by email at cameron_armstrong@ymail.com.